"I won't forget the day I heard that my best friend's daughter had commited suicide. Now his wife, Joyce, has recorded their long, winding journey through grief, fear, guilt, and doubt to healing and peace. The shattered pieces of the Sacketts' lives slowly come back together as time brings healing and as faith in God's wisdom and goodness ultimately triumphs."

— Rev. Herbert Epp

former staff chaplain and director for prayer ministries;

Back to the Bible Ministries

"The suicide of a child is a parent's worst nightmare, calling into question everything that used to make sense in life. Joyce takes us into the deep places of her shattered heart and allows us to navigate this journey of horror and hope with her and her family. There are no easy answers here or self-help mumbo-jumbo. What these pages contain is a candid, faithful witness to the healing power of grace amid absolute devastation and desperation."

— Ronald Scates

senior pastor, Highland Park Presbyterian Church

Goodbye Jeanine

A Mother's Faith Journey
After Her
Daughter's Suicide

JOYCE SACKETT

NAVPRESS®

BRINGING TRUTH TO LIFE

OUR GUARANTEE TO YOU

The Navigators is an international Christian organization. Our mission is to reach, disciple, and equip people to know Christ and to make Him known through successive generations. We envision multitudes of diverse people in the United States and every other nation who have a passionate love for Christ, live a lifestyle of sharing Christ's love, and multiply spiritual laborers among those without Christ.

NavPress is the publishing ministry of The Navigators. NavPress publications help believers learn biblical truth and apply what they learn to their lives and ministries. Our mission is to stimulate spiritual formation among our readers.

ISBN 1-57683-719-X

Cover design by studiogearbox.com.
Cover photo of Jeanine supplied by family.
Creative Team: Rachelle Gardner, Liz Heaney, Darla Hightower, Arvid Wallen, Glynese Northam

Some of the anecdotal illustrations in this book are true to life and are included with the permission of the persons involved. All other illustrations are composites of real situations, and any resemblance to people living or dead is coincidental.

Sackett, Joyce Wilhelmina.
   Goodbye Jeanine : a mother's faith journey after her daughter's
suicide / Joyce Sackett.-- 1st ed.
      p. cm.
   Includes bibliographical references.
   ISBN 1-57683-719-X
1. Sackett, Joyce Wilhelmina. 2. Suicide--Religious
aspects--Christianity. 3. Children--Death--Religious
aspects--Christianity. I. Title.
   BV4907.S23 2005

   248.8'66'092--dc22

                        2005009065

Printed in Canada

1 2 3 4 5 6 7 8 9 10 / 09 08 07 06 05

FOR A FREE CATALOG OF
NAVPRESS BOOKS & BIBLE STUDIES,
CALL 1-800-366-7788 (USA)
OR 1-800-839-4769 (CANADA)

For my husband,
John,
who encourages me every day;
and for our children
and grandchildren.

Contents

The Parable of the Mirrors

There once was a happy little girl, bright and fair, who loved to dance. Her mother and father enjoyed her greatly and often told her how much they loved her. They told her other things that they wanted her to know as well. They told her about God, how he was loving and kind; he made her and she was precious to him, and she should try to be like him in all she did and with everyone she met because they were precious to him too. Then they gave her a book of God's words and told her, "These words will tell you the best way to live, God's way, the way to become your true and whole self."

The little girl loved to please her parents, and she tried hard to please God too. Her heart was tender toward God and generous toward people. She often gave away treasured possessions to those who were less fortunate. But as she grew older and fairer still, she began to build a place inside her heart and surround it with walls. She made this secret place to keep her worries in — worries about her beauty, which was so great and attracted attention that made her uncomfortable. She kept her longings and dreams in this secret place as well. She wanted to be able to fly when she danced, so that those watching would be astonished at her grace. She dreamed of fame, of being rich, of living in a beautiful house with a handsome husband. But she did not tell her mother and father about the secret place in her heart.

As the girl continued to grow more lovely, she began to see herself in two mirrors. One mirror contained God's words, his love, and her family's love for her. These were reflected to her, putting her in the best light, the golden truth-light. When she looked in this mirror, she was filled with happy energy, which made her eager to dance. The other mirror was held by someone she could not see. In this dark mirror she saw her longings for beautiful things and attention and adulation magnified, and she began to believe that they were necessary for her happiness. After a time of standing before the dark mirror, she did not want to dance. She felt sad because the reflections in the dark mirror only made her longings grow and fill up the secret place in her heart.

Time passed, and more and more of the girl's self came to live behind the walls of her secret place. She spent hours pondering the differences between the two mirrors. She began to see that the mirrors were also doors. The golden mirror-door showed a path out of her walled place to an altar where her longings would have to be surrendered. But written on the altar were words of love, words that promised a rising up of her true self from this altar to the golden life where all her longings would be transformed and satisfied.

Through the dark mirror-door she saw people and places and things that called to her, telling her she could have a golden life with them. There was no mention of an altar. She believed she had to make a choice between the mirror-doors, but the decision seemed too difficult. A struggle that began small, with the mirrors, now became great and terrible.

A day came when the lovely girl did not want to think about the choices in the mirrors anymore. The altar had become frightening to her, and she began to hate the dark mirror pictures. Her mind felt painfully heavy, and she was weary of her dilemma. On the day that she was weakest, weariest, loneliest, she made a fatal choice. She created her own mirror-door. In it she put no altar, no things, no people, no places, only peace as she could imagine it, a rest from her struggles.

And she walked through it.

CHAPTER ONE

Death in the House

The Bustle in a house
The Morning after death
Is solemnest of industries
Enacted upon earth —
The Sweeping up the heart,
And putting love away
We shall not want to use again
Until eternity.

—EMILY DICKINSON

It is a Monday morning, and while I am outside in the garden weeding, or digging up a red maple sapling in the woods, our daughter is ending her life. I think she is still sleeping, and so I walk down the hill to the mailbox with some letters. As I walk, a verse from the Psalms comes to mind, "When I am afraid, I will trust in you."[1]

Why am I thinking about this verse? I ask myself. *What am I afraid of? Is it the fact that my mother just had a breast removed? That her cancer may not be licked? That I may not be able to give her the care she'll need? Or is it that I'm dreading the effects in my body from the onset of menopause?*

I think about Jeanine's dark mood of the day before. All day and into the evening she had maintained a scowl and was reluctant to speak to anyone or to respond in conversations around the table. I wonder if her mood will dissipate this day.

I tell God, *I do trust you. I have found you trustworthy for so many years. Where else can I go? You only have the words of life. But I am afraid. Does this mean I'm not trusting? Take away my fears. Give me a peaceful trust.*

I return to the house and go to the kitchen to make sandwiches for Jeanine, thinking that she'll need both a bag lunch to take to her classes at the university and a bag supper to take to her part-time job afterward. All the while I'm singing, "It will be worth it all, when we see Jesus . . ." The song has just popped into my mind, and I wonder, *What will be worth it all? Is this song a message from you, Lord?*

I think of the three concerns that were causing fear in my heart: my mother's cancer, my menopause, and Jeanine's moods. Could this song be alluding to such common troubles? Wasn't its message meant to be an encouragement to those enduring persecution or difficulties much more exotic than mine? I continue to review the lyrics, "Life's trials will seem so small when we see Christ. One look at his dear face all sorrows will erase . . ."

I like the idea that seeing Jesus Christ face-to-face one day will put everything in my life into proper perspective. I sing all the words of the song that I can remember, then go upstairs to wake my daughter. I put my hand on the doorknob, open the door, and find her body but not her self.

Death crams the room. The weight of its presence flattens my lungs. My face is pushed out of shape by its mass. It weighs down the earth, sending the floor away, and I am spun, flung into death's bulk, smothered.

My daughter has tied herself to an upper rung of the ladder to the loft and now her lifeless form lies against the ladder, her toes just touching the floor. I scream, "John!" and my husband comes running to my side, to the room where death is. He lifts Jeanine's body to relieve the pressure of the rope around her neck. I think of running downstairs to get scissors to cut her body free from the rope and ladder, left-handed scissors from my husband's office. I am right-handed. I run down the stairs and then up, amazed that any part of my body can still move, that my mind is still working on so many levels at once. I feel wounded in every bone. Every particle of skin cringes. The tips of my fingers are supersensitive. I feel the steps under my feet, so ordinary a feeling, it seems impossible to allow it. I will stop this nonsense of the ordinary. I will warn everyone in this house, in this life, that the enormous, unthinkable fact in the room upstairs will devour us all.

John tries to revive her, breathing into her mouth, pushing on her chest, but we both know it is futile. All of her life has drained down to her feet. I look for a blanket to cover her cold body. I close her right eye.

Death is the one hideous truth in the room. It has fought with life and won. Somewhere in the foundation of my self, under the floor of my mind, I have stored another truth: God is alive and aware and in charge. Which must mean he is also in this room and that he is stronger and weightier than this mass of death. But my mind feels the pressure of death crowding in. This dead truth covers God's face and swallows him up.

I want to get out of this death room. John wants to hold me and kiss me to stop me from stammering and screaming. I push him away, wanting to go to our bedroom and sit on the floor. I know I am about to die too. Let me sit and try to call on the God of my salvation, the God who lets daughters die. Let him come and get me too. *Take me, God, not Jeanine.*

NO is all I can hear in my head. NO, GOD, NO . . . NO.

Ron Scates, our pastor, is the first to arrive after the paramedics and police. John has called him. *Oh, God! How can we bear it?* Ron! He is still grieving the loss of his two-and-a-half-year-old daughter eighteen months ago!

My mind continues to push away the sickening fact, refusing the knowledge, as the paramedics and police and coroner and the faces of many friends pass before my eyes.

I ask God to tell me what to think, what to do. I don't hear any answer.

Our friend Dick, who lives in Pennsylvania with his wife and family, moves in with us for a few days — Christ-in-Person for us. He answers the phone and the door, takes notes of all the thoughts and prayers and questions of those who call or visit. He becomes a living, loving shield between us and the world. Friends come to hug us, to hold our hands and pray, or to just sit and cry with us.

Salah, another friend, comes each morning — one more comforting presence in our house — to help us make decisions about the funeral and burial. He comes with us to the funeral home and cemetery to deal with the people there. He wants to protect us from the pressure that is sometimes exerted on grieving families to spend a lot of money on caskets and memorials. Salah's wife and son were killed in a car accident just a year ago, so he knows what to expect. His own grief is still so fresh, yet he has strength for us. He also is the presence of Christ to us. He tells us, "God didn't call her, but he was waiting for her."

It helps, somehow, to hear those words.

I lose seven pounds in three days. Meals arrive each day, but I cannot eat. Neither can I sleep. A doctor friend hands me some sleeping pills, which only give my mind a few hours of semi-quiet. When I cannot sleep, I sit at the kitchen table and read Scripture. I wonder briefly at this, that my habit of reading the Bible has not been broken, though I am split and shattered.

I know I am not having a nightmare. My daughter's death is real and final. It will not be undone. I will eventually have to learn to accept the unacceptable truth of her death, but my mind keeps shouting, NO! I tell myself to be still and surrender. I know that if I call on God and address him as Lord, like the psalmist does, then I must be willing to learn to say yes to him, somehow. I must find a way to surrender and listen. And so I read.

The words of the psalms, where fear and hope are mingled, rehearse my own thoughts. I read them out loud, and they are comfortable in my mouth, on my tongue. Each night that I cannot sleep, I sit in the kitchen with God's words and feel some small bit of rest. The psalms hold my heart and keep me from slipping all the way into despair. Grief dangles me over an abyss, but the psalms hold me fast: "I will be glad and rejoice in your love, for you saw my affliction and knew the anguish of my soul."[2]

On the fourth night of sitting and reading, it occurs to me that God knows exactly how I feel. He saw his only son die. He too has lost a child. *Oh, God, thank you for being willing to go through the hell of losing your son. This loss of yours has become my salvation. And Jeanine's.*

But on the following night I do not rise and read when I can't fall asleep. I believe I need to keep trying to sleep, so I stay in bed, but sleep doesn't overcome me. Finally, I push myself away from the pillow, slide my legs over the edge of the bed, and sit there, wanting to be dead. I look down and see that I am sitting on the edge of a well, a deep hole, reaching lower than anyone would ever go by choice. This black hole is as real as the closet across from my bed and the furniture in the room. It gapes at me from the floor. I am on the edge of this hole, and I know I will fall in, and it will mean my death. I feel a pressure behind me, a sense that I am being maneuvered over the edge. This feels like the end of me.

Then I notice something crouching in a corner of our bedroom, leering, sending threats and ridicule out of its eyes at me. Its obscene presence makes the room reek, fills it with filth. This being speaks to my mind about death and the scissors in the bathroom. It tells me what I already suspect, that the scissors are a weapon that will be used against me, by my own hand.

Now I am falling into the pit. I think I am screaming, but my screams do not wake my husband. *Why can't I rouse him to help me in my struggle, to save me from this fall?*

Now, I scream to God, *now, if you are real and you can save, save! I will not survive this fall unless I am saved. If you are not here to save, then there is no living truth, and I must now surrender to death.*

The being in the corner mocks, "Catch her if you can."

I fall and fall, and suddenly I am caught. There is no longer any pit, or any accuser in the corner, only me sitting on the edge of the bed, aware that I am still alive. God must have heard me. He listened and rescued. He holds me and will not let me go. I am no longer sweating, no longer gripping the edge of the bed. I am filled with a confidence that I can put my head down and sleep. I am safe.

Still, for many days after this rescue, I feel afraid when I walk into the bathroom and see the scissors on the counter and remember the threat.

The five of us left in our family sit huddled together in the master bedroom, trying to make decisions about the funeral service and burial.

Julie and Johnny, our first- and second-born, sit on the little couch. My husband pulls up a chair next to them. Joyella, our youngest, and I sit on the bed. We are all uncomfortable, no matter where we choose to sit. We try to take each other's emotional pulse, to hear each other's heart, to comfort and be comforted. We ask questions carefully, speaking in gentle tones. "What kind of service do you think we should have?"

Julie, who has a beautiful, trained singing voice, is willing to sing at the funeral service. I wonder at her bravery. She wants to sing, "It will be worth it all when we see Jesus," the song I was singing just before I found Jeanine dead in her room. The truth of this song is Julie's own conviction. She has loved Jesus and sought to follow him since she was a child. Johnny suggests, "I think we should put *Great Is Thy Faithfulness* on her grave marker."

He is referring to God's faithfulness. Johnny has been a confident Christian since childhood, too. We all agree right away.

We talk about where Jeanine will be buried. Joyella speaks up, "The Memorial Gardens near Dulaney." Dulaney is the high school all of our children have attended, where Joyella is about to enter her senior year. She and Jeanine used to go to this cemetery and walk around. Joyella will pass it every day when she goes to school. "There's a pond there that ducks and geese visit. I'd like it to be near the pond," she says. Again, we all are in agreement. John and I decide to buy a plot large enough for three, so we can be buried beside our daughter when our time comes.

Johnny dares to wonder out loud, "What if Jeanine didn't really want to hang herself? Maybe she was just trying it out, testing the possibility and didn't intend it to be successful. What if she changed her mind at the last minute and wanted to be rescued?"

We all cry over this thought: We did not save her from herself. God knows if she changed her mind. No one came in time to rescue her, to force her to live another day.

The idea that Jeanine might have been hoping for rescue stuns me and opens a door in my mind to a tyrant. Guilt moves in, comes to stay. I begin to believe I am guilty of my daughter's death because I failed to rescue her in her most urgent hour of need. Maybe I have other failures that will be lethal to the other people I love.

Guilt bludgeons the walls of my mind, makes room for doubt. Nothing in me feels strong enough to stand up under the blows. I am afraid that one day all of my inner house will be knocked down and I will be exposed and found deadly wanting. Wanting, because I was not able to keep my daughter alive, because I didn't have a grasp of the deep hurts in someone I loved so dearly. I thought I understood my daughter, knew how to relate to her, teach her, enjoy her. I believed in her good heart and mind, in her desire to grow as a person who sought to follow God.

Jeanine has taken away her life and with it, any confidence I had in my ability to understand God, others, my daughter, or myself. I feel betrayed — by her and by God. If God could give me a song to sing, if he could remind me of a Bible verse to comfort me, why didn't he also spur me to go upstairs in time to save my daughter?

No more will I be able to walk down the hall to her room without shuddering. I tell everyone in the house, "The door to her room must stay open. I cannot ever put my hand on the knob to open the door again."

Death is a closed door. I have no appeal, no way of saying to my daughter, "I'm so sorry for all I have misunderstood. I'm so sorry for not knowing how much you were suffering. Please forgive me."

The shock of that morning when I found Jeanine dead has become a resident snake, poisonous and poised. I am bitten every day. The shock surrounds me with a wall of shudders. Some days I manage to climb up and fall to the other side, but the scenery remains the same.

At the funeral home, we have an hour or so together, just the family, in the room where Jeanine's body lies. I touch her face, so hard and cold. Her hair isn't fixed the way she liked it. She was always so particular about her hair. *It doesn't matter*, I tell myself. John bursts into tears, and we all move to his side and put our arms around him, except for Joyella, who stays beside the coffin.

So many people come to show their support; a line forms that stretches out the door and far down York Road. *All these people care about us? I can't take it in.*

Four middle school girls and their mothers ask to talk with me. The girls had been in a dance class Jeanine taught. We had been warned by our pastor and others that one teenage suicide in a neighborhood or school often begat others in the following months, and I feel anxious about these girls. I think I must give them a warning too. I try to explain how I feel about what Jeanine has done, but I don't know what I'm saying. I see on the faces of these dear girls that I am just confusing them, so I pray silently as I hug each one, that God would help them come to healthy conclusions about suicide and that he would comfort them. As they leave, I feel as though I've missed an opportunity, that maybe these girls wanted to tell me something about Jeanine and I didn't give them the chance.

John is able to talk to everyone. He has the strength to embrace each person in the line, to receive hugs, to share his thoughts, to comfort and be comforted. I endure for a while longer, then retreat to another room and just sit. My brother-in-law comes and sits with me to keep me company.

While we are at the funeral home and later at the cemetery, a deacon from our church stays at our house. This is loving protection for us. Apparently, thieves scout out the homes of those listed in the obituaries knowing the house will be empty on the day of the funeral.

The church is packed for the funeral service. The balcony and breezeway overflow with people. One of the songs we sing surprises me with its strength to quiet my heart:

> *When peace like a river attendeth my way,*
> *When sorrows like sea billows roll,*
> *Whatever my lot, Thou hast taught me to say,*
> *It is well, it is well with my soul.*[3]

I am amazed that I can sing this song truthfully, from my heart, while my mind is in torment. I'm sure I am on the verge of insanity. Maybe this singing and hoping is a farce. I will not be able to endure many more hours of the pain of my loss. But I keep on singing, *It is well.* I feel my innermost self clinging to that confident phrase as the one true truth. I sense within my heart a small but sure belief that the God in whom I have trusted up to now will keep me whole and sane, in spite of my pain.

When our family gets into the limousine to ride to the burial site, we have to wait for a while because the hearse that was to carry Jeanine's body has been sealed shut by the heat of the sun. The electronic keys won't open the doors. So we sit behind smoked-glass windows in the limo and wait for the funeral home to send another hearse.

John wants to get out and talk to people. Many friends have traveled so far to be with us, and he wants to thank them and talk with them.

I am irritated at his ability to relate to so many people in his normal ebullient way. Why isn't he as fragile as I am, as wounded into silence and stillness? Just sitting in the car, hoping I won't burst into screams or faint, takes all the energy I have. I want him to look like a mourner, one of the devastated, like the rest of us in the car. I ask him to stay with us. Is this a reasonable request? Or should the people outside matter more than the way I am feeling? No. We need him next to us, I tell him, more than these friends need to be greeted. When we finally get underway, several hundred cars follow ours to the gravesite.

My mother says, "It looks like a funeral procession for royalty."

Yes. Of course. My daughter is also the daughter of the King of kings.

The graveside service over, we get back into the limo to drive to the church near our house for a lunch reception with our family and friends. Just before we pull away from the curb, Murray Smoot, our pastor emeritus, hands us each a long-stemmed red rose from the flower spray on top of Jeanine's coffin. The rose is perfectly beautiful and fragrant, something tangible to hold onto in this surreal day.

CHAPTER TWO

Grieving Together

Language thou art too narrow, and too weak
To ease us now; great sorrow cannot speak. . . .
Sad hearts, the less they seem the more they are. . . .
Not that they know not, feel not their estate
But extreme sense hath made them desperate.

— JOHN DONNE

It is hard to keep track of time. Has a week really passed since my daughter died?

Our house is overflowing with the flower bouquets sent over from the funeral home. More flowers and plants are delivered to our door. I like having the downstairs full of them. Joyella says she will never like the smell of huge bouquets again. Our church deacons and friends continue to send meals and come by to help clean or just sit and listen. A pile of cards and letters arrive in the mail each day. It takes too much energy to read them all thoroughly, but some I find helpful, like this one, so full of affirmation:

> *We have always looked up to both of you as models*
> *in parenting. We respect your wisdom in handling the*

unique differences in each of your children. The week's
events haven't changed that! We know your children
have always been a priority . . . we will continue to
learn from you . . . we cry with you; we pray with you;
we love you very much!

MARTY AND LINDA

A good friend, the wife of my gynecologist, gives John and me this advice: "Don't neglect each other. Be sure and have sex as soon as you can. You need the comfort of each other's arms. Believe me, it will help."

We take her advice, and I find that the pleasure my husband's body usually gives me is displaced by numbness, seeping out of my heart and taking over every part of me. John embraces me and we lie close, my back against his chest, and I weep for a long while.

My sister and brother-in-law offer our family the use of their apartment in Ocean City, so we make plans to go for a few days. While we are away, friends will come to rip out the loft and the ladder in the room where my daughter hung herself. The ladder was her support in her deed. I insist that it leave the house.

The week we all spend at the ocean is almost comical in its agony. I don't want any of my children out of my sight. No, don't go to the store or to the beach. Or all of us must go together. What I am thinking is this: *If I can see my children, keep my eyes on them, nothing bad can happen to them.*

We talk about Jeanine from time to time or about what we are feeling. But Joyella doesn't join in. She is quiet most of the time. She tells us this much, "I considered Jeanine my closest friend. I felt her pulling away. She shut me out."

We try to encourage her to share more of her thoughts, but she refuses. Later she tells me privately, "It doesn't do any good to talk about my feelings. It doesn't help me."

We all try to be careful with our words, to make them delicate, fitting. No one wants to give anyone else even a tiny twinge of pain. My husband wants to do something, anything, so that he might feel he is fixing our trouble. He wants to mend our wounds with action. "Let's play cards. Anybody want to play cards? Want to play a game? Or how about a walk?"

We try playing some board games, but one by one we admit that we have neither heart nor energy for a game. Joyella speaks up, finally, "Why do we have to do something? Why can't we just be?"

We spend hours just sitting in the living room, leafing through magazines or holding a book in our hands but not reading. Some of us pace the floor or just stand on the balcony looking out at the water. I spend many hours in bed, not sleeping, but with eyes closed, praying for rest.

How does a family mourn together? We cry and sleep a lot.

One evening we all walk down to the beach. My husband and son run out into the water. We women just stand on the beach and watch. In the rough surf, John is thrown down by the high waves, and breaks some of his ribs. Even his physical pain can't rouse empathy in me for my beloved. I am angry with him because we seem to be grieving so differently. Is he grieving? I don't think he feels the weight of my grief, and therefore he can't really help me carry it. How can he play in the ocean like that, seeming like his normal happy-go-lucky self, while I am feeling so numb, severed from who I used to be?

As we all walk slowly back to the apartment, father leaning on son, I am ashamed of my anger and that I don't have any pity for my husband. I feel afraid of the widening gulf between us that I do not know how to breach.

We stay up late talking, discussing our feelings, trying to verbalize the questions we all have about what Jeanine did, what God allowed to happen. John has brought along all the cards and letters people have sent. He thinks maybe we should read them together, a sort of group session, but no one responds to this idea. Joyella sits with us but has little to say — only this, "Why does there have to be so much pain?"

Johnny confesses, "I used to think God was intimate, personal, but now I don't think he cares. He doesn't always do what he says he will do. I feel like he just blew off my prayers for Jeanine." Johnny was actually on his knees praying for his sister right about the time of her death. The night before Jeanine died, John had called him in California where he is stationed with the Navy. When Johnny asked how things were going, his father had told him that Jeanine was not doing well, and so the next morning Johnny prayed for her.

Now Johnny is saying, "I believe God exists, though sometimes I wonder if it's all true. But not believing makes even less sense. I believe and will try to obey, but I don't think God cares about me personally."

I am grateful to the Navy for allowing Johnny to fly home in time for the funeral and to stay with us for a few weeks. Our call to him in California was just in time. His ship was to leave the base that afternoon and had he been on it, he wouldn't have been able to come home.

I begin praying for him, using Psalms 8 and 9 as my guides, that he would be given a deeper understanding of God's ways and a renewed sense of God's love.

Julie's big question is this, "What do I tell my kids?" She teaches music at the middle school in our neighborhood and leads a youth group at her church. She wonders, "What can we depend on to be true about God? Are the mechanics of the Christian life, the disciplines we've learned—spending time with God, reading, studying, memorizing Scripture, witnessing, praying—really going to work for us? Jeanine did all these things. She read her Bible and prayed regularly. She kept a journal, shared her faith with others, went on mission trips . . ."

John doesn't articulate any questions. I wonder if he's thought deep enough to have any. When he tries to tell of his pain, it sounds hollow to me, as though he's merely repeating what others have said.

Back home, we find that the room where Jeanine died has been transformed. Our friends have painted the room a warm peach color and put a leafy wallpaper border around the windows and on the walls at chair-rail height. The loft is gone, but I discover the ladder has not been moved very far. I walk in on it one day, surprised to see it propped up against the wall in the storage shed, intact in its profanity. I back out of the shed, still feeling the ladder's punch to my stomach, and go to John to ask if he would please destroy that ladder. But he doesn't want to. He thinks it's a good ladder; he might use it somewhere later, he says. I tell him what it feels like to have to see that ladder. But it seems as though my pain weighs less than John's practicality. When I absolutely have to go into the shed again, I avert my eyes. I feel the ladder there, but I don't look at it. It punches me anyway while I'm not looking. When I test myself months later to see if I can look at the ladder, I discover it has disappeared.

I feel alone in my grief, shut in to private aching. I don't see anything that looks like grief in my husband, though I do see he is still suffering from the pain of his broken ribs. He tells jokes, which irritates me. I have no energy for laughter yet. He manages things like the checkbook, phone calls, grocery shopping. I barely manage dressing in the mornings.

John is ready to go to church the second Sunday after we return from the ocean. He wants to get back to work, to be with people, to talk about Jeanine's death and how he is learning to accept it. He seems able to talk to almost anyone about it. His arms are open wide to anyone who will enter into an exchange of what sound like banalities to me. I, however, am not able to look anyone in the eye for very long. I don't want to see pity or questions on their faces. I am made of glass. Any heavy word or look might shatter me.

I stay home each Sunday for more than a month.

Some of the cards and letters that have come are balm to my mind. I keep them in a basket in the living room and pick up one or two every now and then and read the gracious, soothing words. Most people are dumbfounded in the face of extreme sorrow. I am touched, grateful for those who reach out to us:

> *We have tried to write during the past few weeks, but the right words didn't seem to come. Sometimes waiting for the right words is not as important as just sharing feelings . . . we think so much of you; we love you and share as much as we can your deep sorrow.*
>
> JOHN AND JOAN

> *We are praying for you, for grace and strength to carry this unspeakable loss . . . we stand in silence next to you, asking for help from El Shaddai.*
>
> LIEKO AND RINSKE

A member of our church who is a professional counselor offers us his time and services, free of charge, for as often as we might want. Our children do not want to go and tell us so in no uncertain terms. I think it wouldn't hurt to go once, but I want to side with the children. John is convinced we should take advantage of the gift, so we go, our children coming along just to please us.

The counselor begins by describing the rings of relationships we all have around us and how, in our grieving, these relationships may help or hurt us: "Here's you in the center and this first ring is your family, followed by these rings representing very close friends, those people you know well. The people in these inner rings will try to say things to you and do things for you that they hope will be comforting. If they fail in this, if they fumble in their attempts to comfort you, that's okay. You know they love you and will try to show it any way they can. But since you are well known in the community, you have these outer rings full of people who think they know you, and some of them are going to wound you. They will think they know what you need to hear, and they will tell you how to grieve or explain to you why Jeanine committed suicide. Just be aware of this and don't take their comments to heart."

He wants to talk about anger next. He asks specifically if we are angry with God, and intimates that we must feel some anger toward God. I think, *Why does he think we need to be angry at God? What does that accomplish? God is who I need now more than ever.*

John says he has no anger toward anyone, but the children admit they are angry with Jeanine for the pain she has caused us all. The counselor puts a chair in the middle of the room and tells us to pretend Jeanine is sitting there. Then he says, "What would you like to say to Jeanine right now?" None of us wants to play this game. We don't say anything.

Then Johnny volunteers this: "It was hard to convince her that I loved her. Whenever I bought her a gift, I had the feeling it had to be an extra special gift in order for her to believe that I cared."

Julie adds, "I always felt I had to go more than the extra mile when I did anything for her, in order for her to believe I was being sincere."

The counselor is having a hard go of it, trying to pull things out of us. I am trying to find anger in me, and I begin to realize it's not anger I'm feeling but anguish that I couldn't keep my daughter from committing suicide. And shame. Shame! I am ashamed that I failed her. What does that say about me? That I feel Jeanine's death puts me in a bad light? Do I care so much about impressions? Is it true that the anguish I feel is not only because of my daughter's despair and my unbearable loss but for my reputation as well? Am I ashamed because I will no longer be considered a good parent?

I suspect this is true. I am horrified at this revelation and don't want to explore my thoughts any longer.

The children think the time spent with the counselor was a waste, mostly, and refuse to return. John and I go to see him once more. This time he wants to talk about how we are managing as a couple. John says he thinks we're doing okay. He talks a bit about how it's been so far, that he recognizes we are grieving at different levels, at a different pace. Then he says something he thinks is funny and laughs. The counselor sees the look on my face and asks, "What are you thinking, Joyce? Look, you have invested a lot in your marriage, like putting money in the bank. It's time you felt free to draw on that account."

I decide to give it a try, even though it doesn't feel right. I turn to John and say what I've said to him already several times: "It irritates me to no end when you make jokes, John. Can't you be serious for a while? Aren't you feeling any sorrow? I hate it when you just go on as if nothing has happened. I am so angry with you."

This is apparently what the counselor is after, as he tries to get me to say more about my anger, to discover the core of it, even suggesting some things I might want to say. But instead of saying anything more, I think about the power of words. I realize that anything I say will be powerful because I have John's full attention. I know I am angry and disappointed in John for not feeling things the way I do, but whatever I say can never be taken back. As I hear my own thoughts I see their absurdity. Of course John and I are going through this horror in very different ways. What did I expect? We are different in so many ways, differences I have found exasperating at times, but mostly differences I have needed, traits so different from mine that I can lean on for support. He's the jolly one, a clown at times — the stable, positive thinker always matter-of-factly trusting in God. He's never met a stranger. Wasn't I drawn to him for these qualities? Why do I insist he be more like me in grief? I need to accept the way he is now, grieving in his own way, and continue to believe in his heart as I've always known it: full of love for God and for me. These thoughts whip through my mind and suddenly I remember the instruction in Proverbs: "reckless words pierce like a sword" and "he who guards his lips guards his soul."

I decide not to just let words fly and say something I will regret later. I don't like it that my husband seems far too lighthearted for the gravity of our circumstances, but why should I wound him? No. I don't have any words I want to hit him with. I won't say anything more.

Please, Lord, don't let our different ways of grieving drive us apart.

One evening, late, John goes outside, walks down our hill to the road below, sits on the curb, and weeps. When he comes back in, I can see he's troubled. He asks, "Am I really fit for ministry? Can I really rule my household well? I certainly didn't do it well on this one . . ."

I hurt for him.

My mother lives with us in a little cottage that John built for her, attached to the west wall of our house. She is grieving the loss of her granddaughter, and she is burdened by my grief as well. Daily she looks for ways to lift my physical load but cannot find a way to ease my sorrow. With tears in her eyes, she tells her sister, "Edna, I see her out there in her garden, and I know she's crying, and I can't do a thing about it."

John and I attend a support group meeting for survivors of suicide. My sister, who has known desperate depression in her own life, comes with us to learn what she can. "Survivors" are those left behind by the one who kills himself. John and I want to learn how to live with our newly acquired title: parents of a suicide. There are no nice words to describe suicide. "She took her own life" is a phrase I've used, which rankles. In the Dutch language, the word for suicide is *zelf-moord*: to murder yourself.

The meeting is held in a church social hall, too large and gray to be comforting. A table against one wall holds some cake, punch, and coffee. Another table, opposite the entrance to the room, has books and pamphlets and information sheets about suicide spread out across it. The titles grab my eyes and seem to shout our misery in the high-ceilinged room: *After Suicide, Lament for a Son, When Life Stood Still, The Fierce Good-bye.*

There are people milling about, some quite young. I wonder if they are siblings of a dead brother or sister. We are a diverse group in the cold room, with only grief in common. A few of us are unsure of the procedure and look around the room for clues to the next best move. Some of the men look as though they have come directly from work in their suits and ties, but most of the attendees wear loose, comfortable, casual clothes. Only their faces reveal their tense and grief-worn bodies. We are invited to sit in a circle on cold, metal folding chairs. Then we are instructed to tell the group, one by one around the circle, how our child or husband or relative killed himself.

"My husband, gun."

"My son, gun."

"My daughter, jump."

"My brother, gun." (Lots of guns: mostly males use guns.)

"My daughter, hanging." I say this. Or is it John who speaks?

We listen to each other's tragic stories. I suspect the purpose of these meetings is to help us stay in touch with our pain, to acknowledge our wounds and fears. I feel the weight of all the grief and pain gathered in the room.

I am startled to realize that John and I are the only ones who think there might be hope of surviving our grief. Maybe our hope is due to our newness to the grief-life. We haven't carried our pain as long as some of the others. Maybe we are still so much in shock that we can't yet know the depth of our pain. Maybe it is too soon for us to be attending such a meeting.

John tries to tell the group about our hope. He tells them that while we don't understand why God has allowed this unthinkable thing to happen, we are confident he can stand up to any charges or questions we lay at his feet. "We are still alive," he says, "though we sometimes think our grief will kill us. We believe our daughter is still alive too, only now invisible. And we will see her again. Our daughter had put her trust in the claims of Jesus Christ many years ago. Her journals tell how much she loved her Savior and desired to live for him. We may never know or understand her reasons for taking matters into her own hands."

"Pain can do that to you," someone in the circle says. Meaning, I suppose, that some kinds of suffering can distort reality and lead to desperate measures.

I try to tell about how I feel after reading Scripture, especially the

Psalms. The Psalms seem to me to be written by someone who can see inside of me, someone who can identify with my grief. Reading them comforts me, makes me feel a little stronger.

John and I exchange glances frequently. We are thinking together: *If only these hurting people could just begin to believe that God can help them, maybe they'd find some relief from their ever-present ache.*

Most of the people sitting in the circle seem so huddled, wretched, and inconsolable. Some of the suicides happened more than eight years ago, and these survivors have been coming ever since. They relive their pain routinely, continuing to pick at their sores. *Is this how it will be for us? God, help us.*

Some of the people thank us for what we shared. We come home restless, drained, and decide not to return to the group because it only seems to add to our misery. I wonder if we came across as arrogant. I worry that we might have offended some of those hurting people.

I am sitting on the floor in the living room with my Bible in my lap, trying to get quiet before God. I feel as though I've been stabbed and the knife is still in the wound. It hurts to breathe sometimes. What's wrong with me? I ask God to relieve the painful sensation in my chest.

I open my Bible and happen to turn to a passage in the gospel of Luke. It tells of the time Mary and Joseph brought their baby, Jesus, to the temple to dedicate him to God. Simeon, a devout Jew who was waiting for the Messiah, meets them as they enter the temple. He recognizes the baby Jesus as the fulfillment of a promise the Holy Spirit had given him, that he wouldn't die before he had seen the Christ. He tells Mary, "This child is destined to cause the falling and rising of many in Israel, and to be a sign that will be spoken against, so that the thoughts of many hearts will be revealed. And a sword will pierce your own soul too."

So Mary's heart was also stabbed. I feel grateful that these words about Mary's pain have been recorded. It makes me feel as though God knows exactly what the wound in my own heart feels like.

I am having a difficult time breathing. It is so physical a pain in my chest that John takes me to the hospital to have a cardiogram and stress test. I am afraid something has broken inside me, or some physical thing is sticking in me somewhere, causing the sharp stabs. After the tests, the technicians tell me my heart is very healthy. They ask if anything had precipitated the pain I am experiencing.

I knew this moment would come. So I try to tell them, though I am feeling the shame again and wondering if they will think it is my fault that Jeanine killed herself. Why is their opinion important to me? Do I believe they will judge me because my daughter killed herself? Maybe I have jumped to conclusions in the past about other people in similar situations. Maybe I have blamed the parents of other suicides. This is a shocking thought, that I might have judged others in this way and therefore assume the same is being thought about me.

"So sorry," the medical technicians all say, "So terrible! Do you have any other children?" these strangers want to know. I think, *Why do you ask? Is that supposed to make a difference? Are you suggesting I can spare one?*

We receive a letter from a missionary friend in China. In the letter, he defines *perseverance*: "The Chinese character for this word is actually two pictures. One is of a man walking. The other is a knife through a heart. Perseverance is simply continuing to walk with a knife in your heart."

I wonder if this is what I can expect: To walk around the rest of my life with this stabbing pain in my chest. But what do I think perseverance means, if it is not pushing through discomfort to get to a desired goal? And what is my goal? To learn to live even though I feel dead, and not to bring dishonor to Christ by whose name I am called.

Why is it necessary to have a sword through our heart? Didn't God see it coming, all this pain, all the problems everywhere? Couldn't he have headed it off, found another way? I don't know. I bring my questions to him again and again.

I read somewhere that the suspicion that God might not be good is the root of all sin. Am I accusing God of not being good because he didn't intervene while Jeanine was securing the rope around her neck?

On Sunday, our pastor uses James 1:1-9 for his text and quotes Billy Graham, who in answer to the question of whether he ever doubted or questioned God, said, "Yes, of course, but I've learned to practice believing my beliefs and doubting my doubts!"

I like this statement. I remind myself that I don't know what God is up to most of the time. Maybe I'll get answers someday. Meanwhile, I want to practice believing my beliefs and doubting my doubts, too. This idea sticks in my mind and I try it out when the questions, confusion, and doubts come sneaking in. Sometimes it works.

The pain in my chest lasts for two more months; sometimes it's dull, sometimes more pronounced. I cry every day. Not all day, just for a bit every now and then. The crying doesn't bring relief, only tiredness.

During my morning reading I come across a verse of Scripture, Deuteronomy 32:3-4, that tells of the good character of my God, and I memorize it so that I will have a weapon against thoughts that arise, thoughts that accuse God of any wrongdoing:

> *I will proclaim the name of the* Lord.
>> *Oh, praise the greatness of our God!*
> *He is the Rock, his works are perfect,*
>> *and all his ways are just.*
> *A faithful God who does no wrong,*
>> *upright and just is he.*

Julie and I sit at the kitchen table and have tea and a chat. She tells me, "I cry when I'm alone. If I had a 'safe' person, someone who understood my grief and who loved me and who wasn't already hurting deeply, I would cry on his shoulder."

Johnny has just called to tell me that he believes in God's love again. I thank God silently as I listen to my son. He tells me he has spent many hours wrestling with his thoughts and questions, praying for faith to believe, asking God to restore in him a strong sense of God's goodness, love, and care. And God has done just that.

"I sent you and Dad a letter all about this, Mom, but I wanted to tell you now."

In his letter, Johnny tells us that he sees his purpose now, in the Navy. It's his opportunity to glorify God. He writes about how he's really motivated to mature as a Christian.

"There are three men here on my ship who say that because of my relationship with God and to them, they have renewed their commitment to Christ."

John reads the letter and beams.

I think it would be a good idea to get a kitten for Lel. (Our nickname for Joyella; what she called herself when she was two.) She has always wanted a cat, but John doesn't like cats at all; his stepmother had eleven of them. I'm more of a dog person, but I believe a kitten would give her something new to do, something to ease the pain in her heart. But will John agree? I sit on the step that goes down to our living room and pray, *Lord, would you help me explain to John why I feel so strongly about getting a kitten? And would you help him to agree? If it's a good idea, that is.*

At this moment John comes downstairs, walks down the hallway to me and says, "Joyce, I've been thinking. Maybe we ought to get a cat for Joyella."

And that's how Jemimah the kitten came to live with us. *Jemimah* means "dove," which is a symbol of the Holy Spirit.

One morning I answer the phone and hear, "Hi, this is Karen. Is Jeanine there?"

I say, "Just a minute," and go to call Jeanine. In the next second, I realize my mistake as I slump to the floor. It takes me a few minutes to pick up the phone again, knowing I will have to tell this girl what has happened. I tell her to please sit down because I have something terrible to tell her. She begins to cry as I tell her, then I begin to cry. She asks if she can come see us. I say yes. Karen is a friend of Jeanine's from school. She has been out of town for a few months and hadn't heard about Jeanine's suicide.

When she arrives, she is still so shaken and tearful. John and I talk with her for a while. I tell her, "I read your name in Jeanine's journal. She has prayed for you."

She says Jeanine had been talking to her about God. John brings out Jeanine's Bible and shows it to her. On the flyleaf is a list of verses titled: "To share with a non-believer."

Karen said, "That's what Jeanine had been sharing with me!"

She takes the Bible from John and hugs it to her chest. Then she asks, "May I go up and just sit in Jeanine's room for a while and look at her Bible?"

I take her upstairs and tell her to take her time, but please leave the door open. About an hour later, she comes down to the kitchen. A visual change has come over her. Her face radiates peace. She seems lit up from the inside. She tells me about conversations she and Jeanine had, about how lost she had been feeling, and how Jeanine had tried to encourage her. She added, "Now I know there must be a God because Jeanine can't be dead. She can't be gone. She has to still be alive somewhere. It must be true."

She asks if she may take the Bible home, just for the weekend, and of course I say yes. The following week her mother calls to thank me for whatever had transpired during Karen's visit to our home. She says, "My daughter is so changed, so at peace with her life. Peace is not a word I would ever have used about my daughter. But she is so changed. I just had to call and say thanks."

I tell her I don't think it was anything I had done or said. It is the result, I say, of her friendship with my daughter.

I have a dream about Jeanine. In the dream, we are sitting on a bed with a few friends, talking. But Jeanine is looking at me with such evil and mockery in her eyes. Her awful expression remains vivid in my mind for days. Never in all her life have I seen such a look on her face. Now her death has given her another face. *What does this dream mean?*

A few days later, I have what might be called a vision of her. I see her clearly. This time I'm not sleeping but sitting in the dining room reading. I happen to look up from my book and see Jeanine coming toward me. The edges of the vision are blurred, so I can't see all of her clearly, just her face, radiant and smiling. She tells me by her smile that she loves me and accepts me. She is standing tall, at peace with God and herself. Her smile and the look of peace on her face remain with me for the rest of that day and the following. I choose to believe it was a vision and call it a gift from God. The bad dream I call a result of grief.

Jeanine's dance instructor at the university calls. She wants permission to dedicate a performance of the Towson State University's dance troupe to the memory of our daughter. They will be performing in concert with the Leningrad State Conservatory. It will be held on Jeanine's birthday and the two nights following. We attend the first two nights.

The program states: Dedicated to the memory of Jeanine Frances Sackett, 1969-1989. Our seats are behind some of the Russian musicians. I love looking at their handsome Slavic faces and listening to their conversation, even though I cannot understand them. Between the second and third nights of the performance, three of these Russians disappear from their group and defect from the Soviet Union. I think, *Oh, Jeanine would have gotten a kick out of this.*

CHAPTER THREE

Don't Be Afraid

No one ever told me that grief felt so much like fear.

— C. S. LEWIS

Fear is all tangled up in my grief. I am afraid that God might allow another unspeakable thing to happen to our family. And I know another fear, deep within me that I cannot give a name to, yet. It has something to do with my feelings of guilt and shame, something about my failures as a mother. The fear is a trembling in my mind and sometimes a sensation in the pit of my stomach, like you get when you are on a roller coaster and you are plunged straight down at great speed.

The evening before she died, I thought of getting up early and asking her if we could spend some time together, to talk and maybe pray. I changed my mind when I first woke, wanting to sleep some more and also not wanting to disturb her because she hadn't been sleeping well over the weekend. Would it have made a difference in her thinking that morning if I had followed through with my idea?

I find my dear husband seated on the love seat in our room, weeping. He looks up at me and says, "God put me in charge of this family and gave us four children to be responsible for. And I've lost one of them." I sit down beside him, put my arm around him and weep with him.

He tells me some more, "My most accusing and awful memory is when you two were sitting on the steps talking, and I walked by. Jeanine's face was full of gloom. She looked so sad. I thought *I ought to be a part of this,* but I didn't know what to do, and you've always had a lot better handle on how to listen and help. And I was thinking about the work that was waiting for me in the office. I had the syllabus to finish, so I could submit it in the morning. . . . I wish now I hadn't let the work pull me away."

"John, I didn't know she was in danger of killing herself! Neither of us knew what to make of her mood that weekend."

"Do you remember, Joyce, the night before, we were in bed talking and praying 'til late, and we said if she doesn't snap out of it in a day or two, we'll get some help . . . and you said, if she should try to kill herself, you'd be so mad at her . . . ?"

I am undone because of what John has just told me. I don't remember saying those words. I can't sit still. I walk around the house in fear, agitated, worrying about what else I may be missing in the lives of those I love. What else have I forgotten — words, thoughts that might have helped save her if I had been really listening to myself?

✳

I worry and pray for our children. Are they grieving in a healthy way? Is their pain from the loss of their sister getting too heavy?

John and I read John Hewett's book *After Suicide* and find this helpful paragraph:

> *Suicide throws a triple whammy on all of you. In the first place, you've lost an immediate family member. This brings a normal amount of grief for you. Secondly, you've experienced the pain and shock of a sudden death. On top of all that, you have to deal with the fact of suicide, with its additional pain and regret. No family is strong enough to ignore that triple shock.*[1]

With this in mind, John and I pray for ourselves and for our children, for protection from the accuser — the one who is a liar and a murderer — and for the presence and comfort of our Lord to be felt strongly each and every day. We pray for the ability to be kind to ourselves and to each other while we heal from this "triple whammy."

I think God wants to say something to all of us in the grief we share. I pray we can hear it. The foundations of our faith have been sorely shaken, but not destroyed.

Friends continue to call or stop by with meals and offers to run errands or do chores for us. They bring books about grieving and loss, pamphlets about how to prevent suicide. The books give little help; I wonder if I will need the pamphlets. People tell us of families where multiple suicides have occurred. I believe they tell us these things out of love and concern, to alert us to the possibility of problems that might be lurking in the minds and hearts of our other children. But such information takes my breath away, increases my fear, and makes me angry that I have to hear such horrible things. Could it possibly be that Julie and Johnny and Joyella will also have suicidal thoughts?

I ask John what he thinks. We agree that the children seem stable to us, that we have nothing to worry about. So we pray for them and for ourselves, seeking to lay our fears in our heavenly Father's lap.

My mind is still searching, probing, peering around corners, lifting lids, and looking under anything that might be hiding that gross flaw in me that caused her death.

The cards and letters pile up. I have several shoeboxes full of written love and prayers for us. Of the hundreds that have come, only one feels like an accusation: "These things happen because we don't listen to our children . . ."

I don't know the writer except by name. She's never been in our home, never seen us relating to our children. I think she is just judging us without knowledge, so I throw the letter away. But I remember her accusation and it becomes a player in the tangle in my heart, a knot of grief, fear, guilt, and shame.

I don't know how to make the knot of emotions go away. My mind keeps whispering that there is something deep in me, some lethal flaw that makes me guilty of Jeanine's death, and I am afraid to face this flaw — afraid too, that others will see it. Jeanine's death has broken me open, and I don't like what I see. I have been so sure of my know-how as a wife, a mother. I have been confident in my ability, honed by training and experience, to understand and counsel others. I have usually felt on top of my responsibilities and have always been careful to project that image. Now it feels as though Jeanine's suicide has revealed me as a fraud and a failure.

I want to be rid of this nagging fear of failure, so I can truly weep for my daughter and not mingle with it any tears for myself. I want to begin again, living as deliberately as I can, doing only what I know is right to do, so I will have no regrets. But even as I write this, I suspect that I won't be able to fulfill this desire.

I continue to read in the Bible each morning and find one day, in the gospel of Mark,[2] a record of an adventure Jesus' disciples had. They are all in a boat out on the Sea of Galilee one night when the wind picks up, and the waves batter the boat as if to break it. This frightening situation continues for a while, when all of a sudden, the disciples see Jesus walking toward them on the water. Now they have a new fear: they think they are seeing a ghost. But Jesus quickly sets them straight by speaking three short sentences: "Take courage! It is I. Don't be afraid."

These three sentences jump off the page to me. I try to relieve my fears with Jesus' words. As I think about the depth of meaning in these three phrases, I imagine having this conversation with Jesus:

"Take courage, Joyce. Courage is available. Reach out for it; take it. I, Jesus, give it to you. I, your Friend and Brother and Savior, am right in the thick of things with you. Don't be afraid. Refuse fear. Believe me, being afraid is not helpful or necessary at this time."

"I don't have to be afraid? Are you saying our future will still be good in spite of losing our beloved Jeanine? And that you will help me to bring to the light those things that I am afraid to face about myself?"

"Yes."

I meditate on Jesus' words for weeks, trying to absorb into myself their truth and power.

John is going to be away for a few days on business. Friends call and ask if I want them to come and stay with me until John returns. I say, "No, thank you. I'm fine."

But I'm not fine. I take John to the airport, and as I begin the drive home, I sense a rising panic. My stomach and the region around my heart start to hurt. I think I might not be able to drive safely. Maybe I will lose my sanity on the highway and steer the car into the concrete dividers in the median. I try to focus on the road and turn on the radio, hoping to hear some word that will rescue me from myself. It is

Sunday, and I tune in randomly to a church service and hear, "Don't be afraid."

The speaker is assuring his audience that in spite of the awfulness of the present situation, or however much turmoil comes in the future, we need not fear. We are greatly loved. God is in charge and has everything under control.

Hang on to this thought, I tell myself. *You are loved. God sees you in this car and has arranged for you to hear again the very phrase you have been meditating on: Don't be afraid.*

I make it home safely but feel too weary to attend church, so I go next door to be with my mother and listen with her to our church's worship service on the radio. Our pastor sums up his message with this phrase, "Don't be afraid." He says that these words are the gospel in a nutshell. I begin to smile and say to God silently, *You are wonderful to love me like this, to listen to my thoughts and comfort me by seeing to it that I hear this message again and again today.*

Later, when I talk to our pastor, I thank him for the sermon that was so helpful to me. I learn that he had not been planning to use the phrase "Don't be afraid" in his sermon. He had penciled it in the margin, decided not to use it, but then at the last minute he put it in. He says, "You must be the reason I changed my mind."

Someone has given us some books and literature to read about suicide and its causes. Thinking it may help to read it all, I come upon some information that makes my heart freeze: Most girls or women commit suicide because of sexual abuse; very often this is abuse by a family member. What? The statement in the literature is a theory based on some studies and observations but is put forth so dogmatically. How can they know? They can't ask the suicide. Could this possibly have been true of Jeanine? That is unthinkable. John? No. Of course not. I know in my deepest heart that John would never, could never, approach any of his daughters in any way other than in a Christ-like, fatherly way.

But what I have read has planted a tiny seed of doubt about my husband, of whom I had never before suspected of doing anything illicit. The need to find out why Jeanine would do something so desperate has grown into something unthinkable. I live with torturous thoughts for weeks, often in such agony and fear that I cannot think of anything else.

I pray and pray, asking God what to do, telling him and myself that it isn't true, wanting to put the thoughts to rest, no, slay them! I feel under attack from the Enemy, the Accuser. My mind runs from one speculation to another, from confidence in my beloved to suspicion of him. I search and search in my memory for anything that might look like a clue to abuse and find nothing.

I feel ashamed that I could ever doubt him, and at the same time I need to ask him about it, but fear the prospect. I want to talk to someone about this, but who? I can't think of anyone I could trust with such thoughts. This craziness in my mind feels just like the craziness I lived with the first few weeks after Jeanine's death.

✳

I tell the women in my Bible study about my anxiety in a general way and ask them to pray for me because I have to ask John a very hard question. That evening as we are in bed, I tell John what I have been wondering because of what I had read. I don't know how I get the words out, and when I say them, they sound unreal, so far removed from the truth that I have always known about my husband.

His answer and the way he answers, with a calm earnestness, begin the removal of all the speculation and fear. "I've never done anything to her, Joyce. I have never touched her in any way like that." He is neither indignant that I have asked nor overly profuse in his denial. Just matter-of-fact, with understanding in his voice. "It's not like I haven't wondered what other people might be suspecting. It seems a lot of people have read such things. But no, Joyce."

Oh, how good he is. How secure. His roots go deep in God. We lie in each other's arms for a while, and I cry and ask his forgiveness for having such thoughts. "Pray for me, John," I say, "that I won't be tortured again like this." I tell him I trust him and can't understand why this had become an issue at all. It must be more of the fallout from our grief.

For the next few days my relief is so great, I sing a lot.

Acknowledge your feelings, people have told us. "Feel them, don't deny them." But it's Jesus who continues to say to me, "Don't be afraid." He feels my pain with me, and he knows my fearful thoughts. I don't think he's telling me to deny my feelings just to adjust my focus and look at him. He and I together will take a look at my feelings of fear and guilt and shame. He will show me the way to get free of these things. He will see to it that I am not defeated in my struggle to hold on to my trust in him.

A verse of Scripture comes to mind, one I've memorized: "So do not fear, for I am with you; do not be dismayed, for I am your God. I will strengthen you and help you; I will uphold you with my righteous right hand."[3]

I want my body, as well as my mind, to get the message of God's promise to me of his nearness, so I take a deep breath, then another, exhaling slowly and completely. (A nurse told me this is a simple way to relieve tension.) And I pray that God will help me let go of my fear.

✳

Someone asks me, "In all your pain, your loss, is God's grace sufficient?"

Before answering I have to think a bit about the question. What is grace? It is to me a strengthening in the core of my being where God speaks his love and understanding to me. And hasn't God been speaking love to me all along in this grief journey? Oh, yes.

I finally answer, "Yes, there is enough grace. At times it may not seem like it when I feel weak, confused, so very tired. But I know it's there, operating on my behalf, because God's Word says so. I'll see more results later, I think."

✳

Guilt continues to haunt me. I writhe under it, so convinced am I of my responsibility for what Jeanine has done. I fling my guilt away, retrieve it, bring it again and again to God. Mothers are supposed to know what's going on in their children's lives and minds, aren't they? Jeanine told three friends she wanted to die, but she didn't tell us. And her friends didn't tell us either. I failed in the most costly, most horrible way. My daughter decided that I could not help her, that I was inadequate. So of course, I am guilty. What I am thinking is this: children of good mothers don't commit suicide.

My guilt has created an idol, the "if onlys." I become fixed on the idea that I have the ability to choose perfectly, if only I would be given another chance! My "if onlys" give shallow comfort, that if I could somehow be allowed to "do it over," I would be perfect in my perceptions and responses and thereby save my daughter. But no. If it were possible to go back and replay the awful day, I would still be just myself, with the same failings and an imperfect knowledge of my daughter and myself.

In light of this bit of self-discovery, it would make sense to let go of the "if onlys" and accept the fact that I didn't know what was in my daughter's mind. But I quickly return to my former lament: *I should have known.*

A few times, I consider that being dead might be more preferable than life, since my grief's pain and fear often feel unbearable. I have made no actual plans in my mind to take my life, but on days or nights when I am exhausted from grieving and fearing, and worn down by shame, the idea of being free of the pain for good tempts me. I wonder if perhaps I am experiencing something of the way Jeanine was feeling and thinking in her last days here. This idea gives me some understanding of her awful choice and a queer sense of identification with her. But for some reason known only to God, and for which I am daily thankful, I do not lose hope that my life can and will be worth living if I can get past the fear and guilt.

I find these words in Erma Bombeck's column in the *Sunday Sun*:

> *Motherhood isn't just a series of contractions. It's a state of mind. From the moment we know life is inside us, we feel a responsibility to protect and defend that human being. It's a promise we can't keep.*[4]

I read in Isaiah 37:14, where Hezekiah gets a threatening letter from his enemy, and he takes it into the temple and spreads it out before the Lord. I love this image. God is so real to Hezekiah, so near. He just spreads the letter out and talks to God about it as if God were in the temple with him. Which he was. And God is in this room with me.

I spread out my fears, my guilt and shame about my failures before him, and he stays with me, assuring me of my welcome in his presence. I have been cleansed, says the writer of Hebrews,[5] by the sacrifice of

Jesus Christ, by his blood, and made clean, white as snow. Amazing chemistry! And God continues to forgive and cleanse as I bring my sins to him in confession and repentance.[6] The Enemy accuses; I accuse myself; but God cleanses and does not accuse me. I am forgiven for all the missed opportunities and misunderstandings.

God, I want the truth of your forgiveness to seep into every crevice of my soul.

I think it is too audacious to believe I can be forgiven for causing or contributing to the despair that led to my daughter's death. But as a friend reminded me, God has already forgiven me for the death of his son, whose death my sin caused. I inhale deeply and imagine drawing into my being all this forgiveness so that it reaches every cell.

Lord, you have thrown my guilt into the depths of the sea.[7]

I read once that there are places in the oceans that are so deep as to preclude ever measuring them. To these deepest parts God has flung my sin and shame and guilt.

John and I are in New Hampshire for a vacation with another couple, long-time friends. These dear friends have recently discovered that one of their sons is emotionally and mentally unstable. He will need almost constant supervision and medication. We grieve with them over this. They are experiencing a kind of death because the dreams they had for their son are dashed, and their hopes have to be adjusted. We cry a lot together. We have good discussions in the evenings, especially around the book of Job, which John is reading through again, slowly.

I listen eagerly to my husband's thoughts and hear more and more of the sorrow in his heart. I am gaining understanding of his grief, and I am so glad for this time away. As John shares about his pain because of Jeanine's suicide, the husband of this couple wants to keep reminding him of Job 42 where all is resolved, healed, made better. But John says, "Yes, but I'm not in that chapter yet. I want to read the process, the journey, then get to the good ending."

When we take walks around the lake, enjoying the autumn briskness and the colors on the trees, I hold John's hand tightly and delight in his nearness, in his freedom to share his heart, in my privilege to belong to him, to be his partner in this walk through grief.

Back home, I find John in tears at his desk a few times. I notice his handwriting has changed, is a bit distorted. He often seems unsure of how to speak to me, hesitating before making even the simplest of statements. Is this because I accused him of not being serious enough? Of not feeling any sorrow? This is such a change in a man who has always been ebullient and carefree in his actions and his speech. I wonder if he is finally feeling his own feelings. Maybe he's been ignoring them while managing the household and our schedules in order to protect me from any more pain. Our family has been the focus of his energy and concern. He's been the strong one, ignoring his own needs in order to undergird the rest of us. Maybe the weight of this care for us is getting too heavy for him. My heart goes out to him and I want to tell him that I know he's grieving in his own way and that I love him.

Maybe tonight I can tell him some of these thoughts, let him know how grateful I am for him.

John and I sit on the terrace after supper, and it seems a good time to talk. He who is the risible one is looking pensive and sad, so I ask, "Tell me what's been on your mind. What have you been thinking and feeling?"

He says he's been remembering the atmosphere in the home and family he grew up in.

"I wanted our family to not be like the one I had—the strife, discord, fighting. I wanted to create a loving, peaceful atmosphere, and I haven't done it. I guess you'd say I feel stunned, and I don't know how to respond to being stunned . . . maybe it's my male ego that keeps saying, you've got to get on with life, keep doing things. Fall off a horse, you get back up. I feel like such a failure. I wasn't able to help Jeanine through her own pain. I was insensitive to how much she was really hurting. I don't know what to think, only that I see how much Jeanine's death has hurt you. You seem so fragile, and I want to do something to keep you from hurting any more, to bring back the joy in our home."

He tells me that he called George, a counselor friend, to ask if he had any wisdom, any ideas on how to handle a family with a loss like ours.

"I guess I thought there must be some formula, some way that I need to be in order to lead the family through all this. Should we sit and talk more, pray together more, what? And George said to just do what comes naturally. Don't push things or try to organize the family to deal with it."

I look my dear in the face and tell him that sounds right to me.

Months go by, and I still find that I am repeating to myself, to friends, "I should have known she was hurting so much. If only I had known the depth of her despair, if only I had gone upstairs sooner . . . I should have known . . ."

Then one morning as I am rehearsing these thoughts to God, I realize that hidden in my protestations is an accusation, a question: *Why did you not make it more clear to me, God?*

My mother and I are visiting friends in the Netherlands. I have prayed that this trip would be great fun for my mother and also encouraging to me. We decide to take a walk along the beach of the North Sea one afternoon. While Anneke strolls along beside my mother, Truus and I walk ahead, talking. She has been a nurse in a psychiatric ward and has some insight into suicidal behavior as well as the reactions of family members after losing a loved one to suicide. I tell her how much it hurts to think that I didn't know what Jeanine was planning to do, that Jeanine told three people that she wanted to die, but they didn't tell us.

Truus asks, "And do you think that you would have less pain if you had known what she was thinking?"

I hadn't thought about it like that. A small light has just been switched on in my mind. I tell her about my battle with guilt, and I keep saying to her again and again, "I should have known; I should have . . . if only I had known, if only . . ." She stops, grabs my shoulders firmly and turns me to face her, "No. You probably couldn't have kept her from doing it, and if you had known, how much more responsible you would be feeling now, how much more pain and guilt. No. God didn't want that. He didn't give you that knowledge. You didn't know. Leave it at that."

I begin to cry tears of relief and gratitude. It's as though Truus has just chipped off a good-sized chunk of the heavy rock sitting on my heart and has cast it into the North Sea. God feels so near. I feel his love, confident he has spoken to me through my friend, as though he is saying, *Rest your mind, Joyce. Relax in me. I am not accusing you.*

Truus and I link arms and continue our walk. With each step I draw strength from her presence and her comforting words.

On another day we visit the Corrie ten Boom house in Haarlem. Upstairs on a table is some free literature. A little bookmark catches my eye: *In het Ja zeggen tegen de wil van God, verliest het lijden zijn macht.* "When we say yes to the will of God, our suffering loses its power."

This thought appeals to me, following on the heels of my time with Truus. I believe God wants me to let go of all the regrets, receive the forgiveness that he has given, and begin to accept my sorrow with a quiet heart. By this means, my Lord can then release me from the power that my grief and guilt and shame have had over me.

✳

I read a lot to distract my mind from dwelling on Jeanine's death. When I find Robert Perkins' *Into the Great Solitude*[8] at the library, the title intrigues me, so I bring it home. In his book, Perkins mentions a plant called River Beauty. I look this plant up in my gardening encyclopedia, which states that it is possibly a form of *epilobium latifolium*. River Beauty is a grayish-green plant with a pink blossom cluster, similar to the primrose. Perkins writes that some people think it tastes like spinach. River Beauty puts down roots along the sandy banks of the Back River in the Arctic. This seems a foolish move to me because the Back River is known for its propensity to overflow its banks. River Beauty may be in bloom when the river rises suddenly, and the high water may last for many days. But this doesn't bother the plant. It just keeps on growing and blooming under water while it waits for the river to recede.

My grief is an Arctic river. In certain seasons it rushes down its channel, gushes over its banks where I live, and flows high over my head. My hair floats. I look around for something to grab. There is nothing. I can only grab my own arms and hold myself. I hope I can remember how to breathe under water. I dig my toes further into the sand. I want to be a River Beauty. Am I blooming yet?

A portrait taken by her friend, Greg, just months before her death. Jeanine's ambiguous expression — a tentative smile, a hint of sorrow — was typical of her.

Christmas, 1987. Opening an "over the top" gift from her brother: real Paloma Picasso perfume, her one big request that year.

A senior in high school, she is in one of her flirty, funny moods.

Dressed for Senior Prom. We bought this fifties gown in a "retro" shop, and she asked me to embellish it with green, her favorite color.

Our happy little dancer, sweet and spunky at age three.

John and Joyce Sackett

"The Princess of Prettiness." Jeanine loved costumes and drama. She, Johnny, and Joyella are ready for "Trick or Treat."

December 1988 — Our last Christmas as a family of six. We're dressed as waiters for a party in our home.

CHAPTER FOUR

My Daughter's Grief

When a person says or thinks, I don't want to live anymore, she may actually be saying— I am weary of dying every day. It is not life she is tired of, but death.

— THOUGHTS GLEANED FROM READING GEORGE MACDONALD

That last evening with her, I wondered what Jeanine was trying to say when she asked, "Did I bring Satan into this house?" What was she talking about? Thinking about it now, I don't remember the context in which she said it or whether I asked her to explain. I guess I was unable to read the dangerous thoughts behind her question. I do remember that I smiled and said, "This house belongs to God, Jeanine. Satan isn't in this house." I was trying to reassure her, hoping she would volunteer some more of her thoughts, but no. I think now my response to her, a dogmatic statement, may have thwarted any discussion.

She was standing in the hall at the foot of the stairs, just staring, looking forlorn. I invited her into the living room to be with the few of us who were sitting around watching a movie and chatting. She declined. Later, Joyella saw her standing there and said, "Come into Dad's study. I'm watching a show you like."

But Jeanine didn't want to. I finally went into the hall and sat on the steps, just to be near her and see if she wanted to talk. This is when she asked me the question about Satan. She also said, "Mom, I've never done drugs. I've never had sex with anyone."

I thanked her for her candor and told her I loved her. I said, " I never suspected you had done those things. Is there anything else you want to tell me?" She just shook her head and then said, "I feel like I can't believe anymore that things will improve for me." This sounded to me as though she was contemplating not believing, but wished she could; so I told her, "I can't believe for you. I wish I could. But you'll need to decide for yourself whether God can be trusted for your future."

After a while, she sat down beside me.

We sat for a while longer; then I nudged her shoulder with my own, hoping to coax her into some more conversation. She gave me a weak smile, then went upstairs to her room.

She was so lonely that summer. Her close friends were frequently out of town, and she was struggling with her jobs and not having any companionship or fun. During the week before her death, Jeanine talked with her youth leader about suicide. She asked him, "Do you think God forgives suicide?" and he replied, "Yes."

Jeanine had told one of her closest friends that she thought about suicide often and that she thought she was having "a nervous breakdown," as she called it. She said she could hear Satan talking to her, deceiving her. Just two weeks before she died, Jeanine and her friend were shopping for bridesmaid dresses, and Jeanine told her, "I'm okay now. I was depressed, but I'm coming out of it. I'm working on it." Her friend believed her.

Weeks after Jeanine's death, her friend told us of these conversations. It occurs to me that in describing her mental state as "a nervous breakdown," my daughter had used the very phrase my family had used to describe the mental and emotional disturbance my father suffered as a result of his time in the Korean War. I was a teenager when he was hospitalized for months because he was so distraught. (Was he suicidal? No one ever said so, but I wonder.) My grandmother on my mother's side also suffered from mental illness and was in a mental hospital off and on most of her life (yet still managed to give birth to ten children). Her sister, my great aunt, hung herself after the death of her husband. This cluster of mental and emotional afflictions in our family history comes to the forefront of my mind.

Is there some proclivity to despair or mental illness in our genes?

Guilt haunts me as I remember what I said to Jeanine one evening while the family was playing a game. She had made a comment in a desperate, funny sort of way that she thought she was "mental." Someone else said, "You *are* crazy!" and I responded jokingly, "Oh, well, it runs in the family."

I would often give Jeanine a hug and tell her I loved her, but sometimes she would get an expression on her face when I did this that made me think she wasn't convinced. I know I was convinced. I loved her smile and spontaneous silliness. Watching her grow and become a young woman gave me great pleasure as well as frequent amusement. At various times in her life, Jeanine wanted to become a painter, a famous actress or dancer, a social worker, or to marry someone rich so she could live in a gorgeous apartment in New York. "High up, so there won't be any bugs or dirt."

I looked for ways to tell her and show her how delighted and thankful I was that she was my daughter. It seemed hard for her to believe me.

Seven months before her own death, Jeanine's friend Paul died. Paul was often at our house, a part of our family life and a friend to all our children. He had been secretary when our son, Johnny, was vice president of their senior class in high school. These two remained buddies through college. Good-looking, fun, thoughtful of others, Paul was also serious about his faith in Christ. He had an earnestness about him, a strong desire to do what he believed would please God. He won a trip to Cancun, Mexico, by selling Bibles between college semesters. It was while he was there in December of 1988, visiting a missionary family and returning from a day at the beach with them, that the Jeep he was driving was struck by a truck and forced over the edge of a mountain road. Paul died instantly; the other three passengers suffered minor injuries.

Jeanine loved Paul. I believe she held on to the hope of becoming more to him than just a good friend. He certainly had an influence over her that John and I didn't have! When she was still in high school, Jeanine dressed in a bizarre fashion for a while, mostly black outfits, ragged edges of fabric, green and black makeup. John and I were not too pleased with the look but tried to be patient (not always successfully!) with this phase of her developing style. Paul happened to be in our kitchen one morning when she came down for breakfast. He took one look at her and said, "You're not going to school looking like that, are you?" She gave him an embarrassed smile, turned on her heel, and went upstairs and changed clothes. That was the end of her Goth phase.

When she began attending college, Paul and Jeanine corresponded. When she was low emotionally, Paul would write letters that buoyed her. She showed a few of the letters to me. In one of them, Paul directed her attention to Psalm 27. At his funeral service, Jeanine read from Paul's letter and shared a spontaneous and touching meditation on this psalm. She was calm and clear-eyed, her words full of assurance and comfort. I leaned into John and whispered, "Will she become a preacher?"

I was so I proud of her that day. I wish I had recorded all she said. I found these notes in her journal, written on the day of Paul's funeral, a summary of what she shared at the service:

> *Paul is where he always wanted to be. . . . He loves the Lord more than anyone I know. . . . Paul is happy right now; he's rejoicing. I want him here, to be with me, to send me encouraging letters, to cheer me up. But if I*

was faced with the choice of being with God or being
here, I would choose to be where Paul is. . . . How
wonderful it is to say with full confidence that Paul
Rodney Kane is with my God right now. . . . I just
praise God that someday I will see Paul again. But
even greater than that, one day I will see God's face.

After Paul's death, Jeanine seemed to have more than her usual amount of moodiness. She was lethargic one day and then pushing herself to be busy the next. We wondered if she was suffering from PMS, so I made an appointment for her with my gynecologist. But more often she seemed her regular happy self, so what does one think? Had I thought she was dangerous to herself, I would have slept beside her, kept her near, counseled with someone who knew about these things.

There was another grief in Jeanine's life that confused her. We had been consulting a sports medicine specialist about the recurring pain in her knees. A few months after Paul's death, we received bad news from this doctor: dancing was putting too much stress on her knees. He felt it would be better for her to cut back, even to stop dancing. But Jeanine loved to dance. She had wanted to take dance lessons ever since she was very young, though she didn't start formal lessons until high school. John's upbringing had given him a negative attitude toward dancing, while I, on the other hand, had taken tap lessons for seven years and still love to dance. It took a while for us to come to an agreement about lessons. Jeanine was an artist as well, and her drawing of ballet dancers forming the word *Dance* was chosen as the logo for her high school dance troupe. In college she had continued her classes in dance, as well as painting and drawing, and was a member of two dance troupes. She volunteered at a nearby school, teaching modern dance to middle school girls.

Yet a month after the doctor's verdict, Jeanine said to me, "Mom, maybe it's a good thing from God that I can't dance anymore because I loved it too much." What? Did she believe that God is miserly with his gifts and grace, removing them in a jealous fit? Or was I just hearing her struggle to accept her disappointment, an attempt to convince herself of some hidden good in it?

If hope deferred makes the heart sick, as the book of Proverbs[1] says, then hope crushed, hope removed, might kill the heart. This is extreme depression. I believe now that Jeanine was mourning the death of her dreams. The death of her dreams meant, to her, the end of her life.

I cry about this, that Jeanine couldn't see beyond her nineteen years, hadn't yet learned by experience to trust God for help in overcoming difficulties. If only she had held on for a while longer . . . then I wonder, how many times before this had she refused to give in to her despair? How often had she made the heroic decision to stay alive until that morning when her courage evaporated?

Why do some people hang on and others lose hope? Those who lose hope brood over disappointments and difficulties, insisting, deep down, on getting their way, even though life is refusing to give it. This disappointment in life, in realizing one's goals are unattainable, may open a door in one's mind to the possibility, the attractiveness, even, of ending it all and being rid of all painful things. The mind narrows itself down to only one solution to all its problems and shuts out any other possibilities. What remains is a desire for a quick fix or a fix at any cost.

On that awful morning, Jeanine had left her Bible on her desk lying open to Psalm 27, which speaks of wanting to be in the house of the Lord. Perhaps this is all the answer I'll get as to why she did what she did: She wanted to be with God and out of her life here. Perhaps she grieved over Paul, over the loss of her dancing dreams, until she thought she could grieve no more, and then took matters into her own hands. When Johnny saw Jeanine's Bible open to this passage, he said, "Look at the last two verses of this psalm, Mom. It says the Lord will let us see his goodness in the land of the *living*! And that we are to wait for him, to be strong and take heart and wait! Maybe Jeanine forgot about these last two verses."

Or maybe her grief kept her from seeing the words.

In those last months before she took herself away, Jeanine had begun to meet with an older friend for counseling and mentoring, and I had hope of her recovery from her frequent dark moods and sadness. She seemed to have this hope too. We talked and prayed and worked at untangling her confused thoughts. I thought we were making headway.

Yet her decision to kill herself feels like a shout of rejection, a final dramatic accusation. But perhaps it is something else—a statement or a question I cannot understand. How can anyone ever know what is going on in another person's mind unless he or she is honest with us about it? Jeanine spoke in code. I did not have the key.

Looking back, so many of the things she said and did the months before she died now seem like huge signposts pointing to her deadly desire. After quitting yet another part-time job to find a better one, she said, "I just don't want people to think I'm a quitter." I told her people wouldn't think that. And anyway, who cares? Part-time jobs are just that. Find one that suits you.

Then there was the time I found her upstairs folding laundry, and she said, "I just want to live here and take care of you and Dad." I laughed because I thought laughter would jar her out of her dramatic, self-pitying mood. "No way," I told her. "You're not going to stay here and take care of us. We'll take care of ourselves, thank you! You need to find your own life."

And then there was that comment she made during a conversation we were having again about her future. School was a burden to her; work was a burden; "I just want to be with God and with Paul."

Now these comments seem like clues, but then, as they happened, they weren't clues. I had no clue. Or I didn't want to believe a clue. I don't know what the truth is. Saying I didn't want to believe she was suicidal makes me feel even more culpable. But I didn't know. If I look further back, when she was in high school, I remember other things that contribute now to my sense that she was sending out signals all along, but none of us knew how to read them.

One time when she was in the kitchen fixing lunch, she said, "I wish I could cut my breasts off."

After I swallowed my shock, I asked, "And why is that?"

"My dance teacher says I'm too 'built' to be a good dancer, at least not a ballet dancer, anyway."

"And do you really want to become a ballet dancer?"

"I don't know . . ."

I remember telling her that her beautiful body was a gift, and she was a delight to behold, but that didn't cheer her up.

Did my daughter mean to accuse me in some way by her means of death? One counselor suggested that it was an angry thing to do, a way to express her anger toward us by killing herself in our home. But none of us in the family believe that. We're certain Jeanine just did not want to be found by anyone else but us. We think she trusted us to treat her body with respect. She couldn't count on the actions of others who might discover her body somewhere else. Of course, in her distraught state, she couldn't foresee the nightmares and daily shudders I would have because my mind cannot forget what my eyes saw that morning.

In her journals written during the months just before her death, I find page after page of comments on passages of Scripture she had read. And below her thoughts, a prayer to God that she composed each day.

In several of these prayers are words of thanks to God for her family.

Just a week or two before she died, Jeanine told a friend that John and I were "never more there" for her, that we were helping her in so many ways. When we hear later about this affirmation of our parenting, I dare to think I can let go of my guilt. But it will not let go of me.

I begin to remember details of Jeanine's life in which I see myself as seriously lacking in understanding and compassion. When she was about twelve, I was walking by her bedroom and overheard her telling a friend that she had been raped. I stopped at her door and said, "Jeanine, you weren't raped!" I was incredulous, thinking that I knew the situation she was talking about. It happened when she was five. It was "against the rules" to go into someone's house if the mother wasn't home, but our neighbor's teenage son had enticed her into his house with candy, undressed her, and then laid on top of her. His younger brother interrupted him, and she came back home and told me what had happened. As I questioned Jeanine gently that evening about the incident, she didn't seem frightened or in any distress. Based on what we could ascertain at the time, she hadn't been injured in any physical way. I knew nothing then of the emotional devastation and long-lasting damage caused by any sexual violation.[2]

So because of what I thought I knew of my dear Jeanine — her love of drama and display, her need for attention — when I overheard her comment to her friend, I corrected her. I embarrassed her in front of her friend, and what's worse, I believe I wounded her deeply and missed a huge opportunity to listen and see that awful violation through her eyes.

When I think of it now, I am appalled at my lack of wisdom and sensitivity. Would that I had asked her some questions instead of embarrassing her in front of her friend. Would that I had asked her to tell me about the time she was referring to.

I don't remember what else was said, only the embarrassed and confused look on her face. I search for a memory that will make me feel better about myself, make me look good in my own eyes, but I find none. I was no comfort or encouragement to my dear daughter who was hurting in a way I hadn't begun to understand.

How many other times had I misread her and been insensitive, thereby giving her reasons to doubt herself and hide her desperation? If only I had been a better person, more sensitive to her feelings, would Jeanine still be alive?

Sometimes in my reveries I am so overcome with feelings of guilt and unworthiness, I fear I may not even approach God, may not ask for help. I need to prepare a talk I will give in a few days, and I cannot even pray. I sit with the devotional guide I use, *Daily Light,* open on my lap and try to read. All at once I have a strong sense that I ought not to read this morning's verses. It's as though I hear a voice in my head saying, "Turn back the page." It's so compelling a thought, I turn back to yesterday's reading, and the first thing my eye rests on is a verse in the evening reading section, one I hadn't even looked at yesterday: "Woman, where are your accusers?"

I wipe my eyes, so I can read again with confident delight that I am fully and warmly accepted in God's presence. Oh, how I need to be reminded of this again and again. I've asked for forgiveness for anything I may or may not have done to injure my daughter in any way, and God is once again telling me, *Yes, of course. Jesus paid your debt. Come here. Come near.*

It seems to me that God is also responding to the turmoil in my heart through the cards and letters that continue to come from our brothers and sisters in Christ. They contain comforting words that feel like they have come straight from God's heart to mine:

> *God loves her and she loved him. Suicide is a difficult thing to understand theologically, but she is with him because she belonged to him — this the Bible confirms. You are not at fault. Every one of us parents feels we could always do more — but we have loved, cared, and given. You did so much more than most.*
>
> PAUL

> *There seems to me no deeper trial for loving, conscientious parents to endure than the death of a beloved child, and no greater tragedy than loss of that child by suicide. The temptation for self-blame is overwhelming, the desire to "rerun the tape" and divert the story at some critical juncture never dies, and the sense that you somehow could have made things "more right" burns constantly in the back of the mind,*

pulsing through your very veins with every heartbeat. But I'm increasingly aware that suicides do not occur predominantly in homes where people are nasty, where love is unknown, and relations are poor. Two of the kindest, gentlest men I know have lost their wives by suicide in spite of great effort to prevent it. Jeanine's terrible death reflects internal terror or despair, not the failure of a loving Mom and Dad to demonstrate their love. I pray that as you struggle through the darkness of this terrible experience, the agony of your loss will not be compounded by the anguish of incorrectly assumed responsibility and unwarranted guilt, and I pray God's strength for you.

Bart (and Dori too)

This letter is a special treasure to me. In it I find understanding: feeling like a failure is a normal reaction to suicide of a loved one. I find, too, a strong assurance of love and support. I may accuse myself of having played some part in Jeanine's death, but our friends do not. I read and reread these letters. It is obvious that God knows my every thought and sees to it that I receive such specific and gentle comfort.

I have just read a true story about Fred Davis,[3] a policeman in North Carolina, whose teenage daughter shot herself in their home after breaking up with her boyfriend. Fred decided he didn't want to live anymore either, so convinced was he of his guilt in her death. He planned to ram his car into a concrete wall, but as he was driving to it, saw a group of young girls standing on the highway and stopped to inquire. They said their car had stalled, so they piled into Fred's patrol car, and he took them to their car which was parked right in front of the wall he was going to smash into! These girls seemed to know about his trouble because they gave him a Bible (they were selling them door-to-door, they said) with a ribbon in the portion in 1 Thessalonians about the Second Coming and the safety of those who have died in Christ. Fred recognized the presence of God on that highway and surrendered his life to him.

I think those girls were angels, and God was doing something special that night, on that highway, for a severely wounded soul, the parent of a suicide. This story astonishes me. God didn't rescue Fred's daughter, but he kept Fred from killing himself. That's definitely the way Fred saw it, according to the story. Faith tells me to trust that God is always up to something good, no matter how it looks at the time. I do so wish Jeanine had been rescued. But now I will just wait and see what God is up to this time.

Luke 15:20 says: "While he (the son) was still a long distance away, his father saw him coming. Filled with love and compassion, he ran to his son, embraced him, and kissed him" (NLT).

I like to imagine, Lord, that this was your loving response to our Jeanine. Was Jeanine thinking immediately after her deed that she had deeply wounded you, Lord, and all of us? Did you hug and kiss her and welcome her? I hope so. I believe she is with you now, safe, forgiven of what might have needed forgiveness, enjoying your arms around her.

CHAPTER FIVE

Grief Upon Grief

On the first anniversary of Jeanine's death we receive letters from some friends who truly understand our heartache and remember the significance of this day:

> *Hardly anything makes me love Jesus more than his gasping, [as he hung on the cross]'My God, why . . . ?' Nothing in Scripture underscores his total humanity and identification with us and our dreaded mortality more than this moment of awful weakness and darkness. And only Almighty God could bring himself to such an identification. 'But for the <u>joy</u> before him, he endured. . . .'*
>
> *Jeanine has now spent a whole year in that wonderful Presence. Each of you—John, Joyce, Julie, Johnny, and Joyella — will suffer through this in your own private way, but my prayer today is that the joy of hope and the hope of joy will ultimately carry the day.*
>
> JOHN MURRAY SMOOT

Our hearts continue to go out to you and your family over the tragic loss of Jeanine. We have joined the literally hundreds of folks who are praying for you all.

There may be times when you will find some of the same nagging questions coming back to you that you thought you had dealt with, like . . . what could have been done differently . . . why . . . etc. This is one time when being professional people can cause you grief because you think you are supposed to know the answers to these kinds of questions. . . . We know of no more loving family than you all have been, are, and will continue to be. You did all you could. Still, death hurts like hell . . .

ALEX AND PAT

I am so weary of my grief. But God is giving me these gifts of hope, and it makes my heart glad to think about this: I will one day join God in enjoying my daughter in his heavenly kingdom. As I read and reread these and other letters, I weep, overcome with gratitude to God for giving such healing words to so many of his people.

Grief is becoming a way of life. We receive word that my brother has taken his life. He shot himself in front of his wife. John is in Colorado when the call comes, but Joyella is with me and begins to cry. "Oh,

Mom," she says, and I see fear on her face.

"Are you afraid for me?" I ask, and when she says, "Yes," I assure her that I will be okay, though I notice my hands are shaking, and I am too weak to walk for a bit, but I must go next door and tell my mother. But first I call John.

"What shall I do?" I ask him. "Mom is asleep. It's nearly midnight. Should I wake her?" John thinks maybe I should let her have a good night's sleep and tell her in the morning. I realize we are having the most inane conversation because we are both befuddled, knocked sideways by this appalling news. I can't imagine going to bed with this horror on my mind, anticipating giving Mom the news in the morning. I am shaking and feeling the fear again.

I call my sister and tell her about Gordy. Her voice tells me she is about to have hysterics. I ask her what she thinks I should do about telling Mom. She swears at me in her anger at this news. While I'm on the phone with her I see outside some policemen walking around the house with flashlights.

"Oh, policemen have arrived," I tell Jeanette. "I must go. I have to be there with Mom when they knock on her door." My brother was a policeman on the SWAT team for the county.

My mother is frightened when she opens her door to three policemen and me. "It's Gordy, isn't it?"

When I give her the dreadful news, she has a heart attack. The paramedics come, and off we go to the hospital where Mom is diagnosed and told she must have heart surgery, a triple bypass. She will not be able to attend her son's funeral.

John and I take care of the details of the church service and burial. My mother says to me, "I never thought you would be comforting me for the same loss you had."

I go to see her in the hospital every day for a month.

I visit my brother's wife and see the hole in the wall where the bullet went through. I have no strength to give to her. I try reading some verses from the Bible to comfort her, then we weep in each other's arms. I drive home slowly because I cannot see very well.

I don't know how to grieve for my brother. I am saddened and dismayed by the thought that he was in such dire straits, that he was so full of anger and despair as to do violence to his wife as well, by committing suicide in front of her. This is far too horrendous to think about. I think about the pain he has also caused his first wife and their daughter. I weep over his coffin, but I sense that my sorrow for him will be short-lived. It seems small when I measure it against my grief because of Jeanine, the loss above all losses. I think the wound from her death will remain the wound next to which all other suffering will seem slight.

A year passes, and my mother dies suddenly. We return from shopping for ingredients for the Christmas baking when she begins to feel ill. She starts having difficulty conversing and focusing her eyes (she is on the phone with my sister when this happens, who alerts me), then begins to vomit. Our doctor says to call 911. While I wait for the paramedics to arrive, I give my mother a little pail to vomit in and stand across the room from her, leaning on the counter, so afraid. I don't want another crisis, and this looks very bad to me.

God, what do I do now? All the fear is coming back, all the agony. God, please. I need my mother. She's my cheerleader.

The same paramedics who came when Mom had the heart attack last year show up again to help. They are so tender and gentle with my mother that I am encouraged to think, *Yes, God is here; God is aware and caring for us.* At the hospital, Mom enters what appears to be a dreamlike state. Occasionally she whispers something, and I bend my ear to her mouth to hear and understand, but the words are barely discernible. John joins me at the hospital; my sisters and their families arrive. Our pastor comes and prays with us around Mom's bed. Before I learn what is happening to her, I think she is having a stroke, and so, standing by her bed, I begin praying for the strength to care for her.

I know becoming dependent will be a great trial for her. My mother never wanted to be a burden. She was always the load-lifter. I used to tell her she made me look good because she often ironed for me or cooked or helped with the cleaning.

Help me, God, to be what I need to be for her. . . . God, what are you doing?

High blood pressure has burst a vessel in her brain, and she is hemorrhaging. She dies peacefully in the morning.

The pain around my heart has returned. I am in a fog. Who can get used to death? Morticians? Gangsters? Cops? Death leaves a blank, creates a black hole where someone fell in. Who can get used to this sucking away of life, the disappearance of warm, moving flesh? My daughter is not coming back. And now my brother and my mother are gone somewhere else forever.

Job was able to say, the Lord gave, and the Lord has taken away; may the name of the Lord be praised. Will I ever be able to say this and mean it?

All our children are home with us to attend my mother's funeral and because it is Christmas. We gather in the living room each evening and play Christmas music as we talk or work on a puzzle. It's as though we feel the need to be close together, to close ranks against any more losses. One song on the Christmas album I have a hard time listening to: "All Is Well." The melody is beautiful and haunting, and I know the words are truth, but this song moves me to tears, copious and long-lasting weeping, every time it is played.

All is well?

Is this what you call well, Lord? How can I stand it? Let me feel that these words are truth. I believe them, but I can't feel them. Please show me more of your kindness; give some blessings that are easy to bear!

Murray, our pastor emeritus, tells us that when he heard of Mom's death he said to God, "Enough!"

Oh, how I love this man who carries our burdens as his own and dares to defend us before the throne of God.

I try writing to find out where my heart is, to unburden myself, to see if my thoughts about God and my grief are becoming untangled:

GRIEF WORN

I'm wearing a dress that doesn't fit. I can't take this dress off. I must wear it all the time. It's not my color or style at all, it is rough, dark, ugly. It has no buttons and seems to be sewn to my skin and my heart. It has a bodice that threatens to cut off my breathing. This dress covers every inch of my body, and I trip over its length. The sleeves hamper my hands. The collar flies in my face, and I cannot see.

Oh, Lord God, help me to undress.

But I know this is not the right prayer. God has given me this dress to wear. He designed it from cloth that had been thrown over me by the Enemy who wanted to smother me. God caught the bolt and instantly adjusted it to fall over my head.

He will help me to wear this dress. I can feel him

making alterations already. He's going to fold back the sleeves and free my hands. He will loosen the bodice, and I will be able to breathe more normally. Knowing him, I can expect this dress to be transformed into a gown. Meanwhile, my tears keep the shoulders damp, and I secretly pick at the threads, hoping they will unravel. I tell myself: let God do the changing. His designs are always exquisitely fitted. And I ask him for help to keep walking with this tangle at my ankles.

If, Lord, you never explain to me why I had to put this dress on, I will still trust your judgment. I know you love me. Your love is designing something far more beautiful than anything I would have chosen. You will change this distressing dress into a garment of rare beauty, lovingly suited to me. You have promised to do this. I believe you. Thank you.

I am reminded of a dialogue Teresa of Avila had with God. She had to cross a river and was having trouble, not only because she was very old but sick as well. She complained to God that because of her difficulties, she couldn't quite enjoy the scenery of her journey. And God said to her, "This is how I treat my friends," to which she replied, "Yes, Lord, and that's why you have so few of them."[1]

This recollection makes me smile a bit. If old Teresa could get through her troubles bravely, victoriously, and with wit, maybe I can too. This idea, that God's friends are the ones he can trust with adversity, intrigues me. I gave my life, my self, to him long ago and told him I would go anywhere, endure whatever is necessary so that others might see him in me and thereby become his followers as well. It just might be that God is taking me at my word, trusting me to live through intensely difficult circumstances because I am his friend and because he is accomplishing something in our lives that will have eternal significance for many.

I find an article in the newspaper about a woman who opened her own beauty shop eight years after the death of her only son. It took her that long, she said, to get her strength back. Will I ever feel strong again? I guess I'll need quite a few years to get my strength back after so much grief. And maybe strength never fully returns. I've been growing older while I've been learning how to live with my losses. I can't expect to wake one morning and think, *now I'm my ol' self again*. Maybe I'm growing into someone better, deeper, wiser.

Perhaps some kind of cosmic struggle is going on, and it is being played out in my life. And God is somehow praised each time I choose to trust him instead of jumping ship. In this severely damaged world, maybe I can only really grow up, get healed, and get close to God through suffering. I don't like this formula, but I want to learn how to accept it. God's Word is full of references to this principle: We must struggle and suffer and thereby be changed, our character strengthened, our likeness to Christ increased. And a reward is waiting.

I continue to think that God has to be doing something so amazing in our lives, and perhaps in the lives of others, that all this loss and grief have been allowed for a huge and holy purpose. On the other hand, all people everywhere suffer loss and pain. Christians aren't exempt. The difference for us, though, is that we have Christ in us and at our elbow, walking through the awful things that come our way. Our Lord Jesus bears it all with us and promises to bring us safely home to him . . . in his time . . . in his way . . . for his glory. Great gladness is in our future.

For now, Jeanine's death remains an unthinkable loss; my brother's death, a tragic result of his dangerous and desperate choices; my mother's death, God's conclusion to a well-lived life.

The tears Jesus shed beside Lazarus's grave show me how this ruined world affected him too. He wept even though he knew that the sad present, the undesirable and often unbearable reality, will one day be swallowed up in the one and only reality: eternity in God's presence. No pain, no tears, much laughter. What a picture! A weeping God. God expressing his heart of compassion for us in salty tears running down the face of Jesus. No other god weeps, is wounded, dies. Jesus is the only one who can truly comfort us because he knows what it feels like to suffer and grieve:

We must have Thee, O Jesus of the Scars.
The other gods were strong but Thou wast weak;
They rode, but Thou did'st stumble to a throne;
But to our wounds, God's wounds alone can speak,
And not a God has wounds but Thou alone.

ANONYMOUS

When I think about what's to come, the fulfillment of powerful promises, I begin to understand why Jesus encourages us over and over, saying, "Don't be afraid." Of course. Let your mind go to the conclusion or rather the new beginning and see that though grief is inevitable now, it is redeemable. And fear isn't necessary.

CHAPTER SIX

Surviving Memory

*In our sleep pain which cannot forget falls drop by drop
upon the heart until, in our own despair, against our
will, comes wisdom through the awful grace of God.*

AESCHYLUS

It still sneaks up on me, the memory of finding her dead. After the shudders pass and I suppress the scream rising in my throat, I unsteadily step around the memory, knowing I must absorb again this immense fact of my life. Is it possible that one day I will be surprised by this awful image and yet not feel faint?

I guess there are as many ways to live with grief and pain as there are people. A friend told me about her sister, whose husband had died. As a new widow, she seemed to be coping well in spite of her loss. She was comforting her family and friends, running her household well, and managing her other responsibilities. My friend asked her sister how she was able to be so strong while her grief was still so fresh, and she replied, "I have walked the length of my lawn countless times, beating the trees with a stick."

It feels like I'm beating myself with a stick each time I begin my litany of regrets and self-accusations. But I don't cry hard anymore nor very often. Tears leak out at times, though, unexpected, prompted by a song sung at church, a face seen in a crowd, or a memory wafting through my mind.

Actor Paul Newman lost a son to a drug overdose in 1978. In an interview in 1994, Newman was asked about how he was dealing with the loss, now that so many years had passed. He said, "It never gets any better. It just gets different." Yes. Jeanine's suicide will always be a huge and horrifying fact in the story of my life. But some days it seems to have been wrapped up a bit in something soft and set on a shelf somewhere in my brain.

Joyella and I are talking about my writing, and she tells me she wishes now she had kept a better journal during and throughout her grieving. She would like to remember more of her thoughts and the things she learned in those sad days.

But then she says she didn't want to write about Jeanine's death because that would make it seem more real: "Sometimes it's easier to pretend when there isn't hard proof. In twelfth grade English there were times when we had to just write, about anything. It wasn't graded, just counted for participation. I remember writing about Jeanine's suicide as if it had been a drug overdose. That was easier for me to deal with.

In my story, we find her collapsed on the floor, with an empty bottle of pills. She is not dead. After being taken to the hospital, we discover she is in a coma and not expected to survive. Eventually she dies, but in my story, I have a chance to say good-bye, and tell her all the things I wanted to. I know she cannot hear me, but somehow it helps. I wish it had happened that way; it might have been easier for us. But then, again, it still would be awful."

Jeanine's best friend, Kellie, sends a bouquet of flowers every anniversary of Jeanine's death, as well as on Jeanine's birthday. I think it is Kellie's way of relieving her own pain of losing a best friend.

"After all," Kellie says when I call to thank her, "it's Jeanine! How could I ever forget!"

I'm so glad for the flowers on the anniversaries when I am feeling my loss intensely. But sometimes I do want to forget. The flowers arrive, and I'm surprised because I hadn't even realized what day it was. I wasn't feeling sad at all, and then the flowers remind me.

John and I are in the Netherlands, staying with Bram and Anneke in Middelburg. Bram has been faithful to pray for us throughout our ordeal. Bram tells us he prayed that God would see to it that Satan would sorely regret what he did to Jeanine. His prayer reminds me of another friend who, when entering the church and seeing Jeanine's coffin there, was overcome with sadness and then felt a rising hatred for Satan who is the Destroyer. He told us later that he committed himself anew to helping rescue others who are in despair. Such expressions of identification with us give us comfort and renew our courage.

Anneke and I take a long walk along the canal and around the market square. As we walk, she tells me about her grandmother, her Oma, who lost a son many years ago. He died when he was ten years old. Anneke's Oma is now eighty-four years old, a happy, alert, and busy woman, involved in the lives of her fourteen other children and her many grandchildren. But still, she tells Anneke, she thinks of her son who is dead, every day.

It's the same for me.

I glance at Jeanine's picture, and my brain tastes salt and gall. I'm thinking of taking the picture off the piano. When people who knew her come to our house, they see the picture, and I see on their faces a pang of grief or merely embarrassment. They are reminded of our grief and don't know how to "be" around us. Or if someone comes who didn't know her they might see the picture and ask, "Who is that?" and I will have to tell it again. I don't want to have to tell it again. I'll put the picture away. Is this denial or survival?

What has just come to mind is the time Jeanine asked, no— demanded—that we sit and listen to her. I think she was about seventeen at the time. She needed to tell us something. The atmosphere was charged with accusation and anger, even before she spoke. John and I sat together on our bed, leaning against the headboard, and gave her our attention. Jeanine sat in a chair at the foot of the bed and began to scold and question and accuse us. Funny, I can't remember her actual words, only the strength of her conviction that we were terrible parents, that we had missed opportunities with her, didn't care about her. Such things she said. I think she felt better after getting it all off her chest, but I certainly didn't feel any better afterward. Remembering that time, I accuse myself now for not knowing who she really was, for being so out of touch with her that I couldn't see her anger until it spilled over.

Our other children disagree with my assessment of our performance as parents. It helps to remember that. And I remember that when Jeanine's counselor heard what she had said to us, she told Jeanine that they couldn't meet again until Jeanine apologized to us for her conduct. Which she did.

Sometimes I write letters to Jeanine. Or I imagine being able to talk to her. I say, if you were still here, we could have some fun. We could visit a museum or go shopping for quirky fifties dresses. I could watch you dance. I could listen to you as you try to explain your latest passion.

After attending a staff conference at Asilimar, a conference facility in Monterey, California, John and I are spending two days at the Gosby

House in Pacific Grove. This is a beautiful bed-and-breakfast on the main street. This morning, a cool morning, we have our breakfast in the cozy fireplace room, where I notice a mother and daughter at a nearby table. The daughter, maybe thirteen or fourteen, is sipping tea and staring into the fire. Her large, green eyes remind me so very much of Jeanine's. I watch the mother talking to her daughter, patting her shoulder. I look at the girl's lovely eyes and feel heat rising up behind my own, bringing tears.

As John and I take a stroll afterward along the water's edge, I see a young woman with a backpack slung over her shoulder, one like I see so many students carrying now. Would Jeanine have a backpack like that if she were still here? Or would she make do without one because they're probably expensive, and she didn't have much money for extras. It gives me a pang of sadness, thinking about Jeanine's struggles to make ends meet financially that summer. Could we have helped her more, sacrificed more?

I keep trying to get past the pain so that memories can be fun again. I want to think of how spontaneous she was, how graceful when she danced, how uninhibited and unpredictable, how funny. Didn't she always have the most outrageous Halloween costumes? She turned herself into a California raisin one year, by stuffing a large black trash bag and wearing it with tights and black face makeup. Another Halloween she was Mr. T., and I want to remember how beautiful she was. Most of the time, when Jeanine comes to mind, I have to wade through the horror of how she died and push past the shudders to the sunny side of memory.

When Jeanine was a bubbly, flirty, funny three-year-old, I would often play a music tape that she enjoyed. Friends in New Zealand had sent the tape to us while we were living in the Philippines, but the singers' names and the source of the music is long lost, along with the tape, after so many moves. Jeanine's favorite part on the tape was a chorus based on Psalm 30:11, set to a lively beat:

> *Thou hast turned my mourning into dancing for me.*
> *Thou hast put off my sackcloth. Thou hast turned my*
> *mourning into dancing for me and girded me with*
> *gladness; to the end my glory will sing praise unto*
> *Thee, and not keep silent; oh, Lord my God, I will give*
> *thanks unto Thee forever.*

When Jeanine heard those drums and the music, she would come running from wherever she was playing to the room where I was. She'd begin to wiggle and dance and grin at me, enjoying the drumbeat and my full attention.

I told this memory to a friend, and she said, "Joyce, it sounds like God was already comforting you way back then." I choose to believe this. This has got to be a God-thing, not a coincidence, that the song and tune Jeanine danced to when she was so small would become a personal promise, and her dancing a sweet memory.

One of my friends assumed that we would have to move from this house because of the unthinkable thing that happened in it. That idea hadn't entered my mind or John's. When someone suggested to John, early in our grieving, that we would no doubt move, he replied, "No. Jeanine has already messed up our family. I won't let her take away our home too. It would feel like a retreat in the face of a spiritual attack."

Blessing Hill is our home, 1.63 acres on a steep hill in Timonium, Maryland. It was once a stylish riding school and stables. We converted the stucco barn into a house with a lot of help from our friends. It contains the unique expressions of our family's talents and pleasures. The following letter is one of several that affirmed our conviction about not moving:

> *What a blessed home the Lord has enabled you to create . . . indeed it is and will always be "Blessing Hill." There is peace and healing in this house — and I pray that it is not so familiar to you that you cannot sense the refuge God has built here.*
>
> HEIDI

It occurs to me only occasionally, as I sit here to think and write, that I am on the exact spot where Jeanine was last alive. I don't sit here because of that fact. It is simply the best spot for my desk. I sit here for the light and the view to the east from the window near my right shoulder. I can see our lawn and woods. Sometimes I see deer browsing along the boundary hedge. So much that was original to this room is now gone. It is now a wonderful place in spite of the unthinkable thing that happened in it. The large slanted window on the south wall brings in the sky and sunlight. I feel as if I'm in the treetops when I sit under this window to read and pray each morning. I keep plants on a marble shelf here. Yellow freesia, purple orchids, and red geraniums are blooming now. This is a light and airy room. When I walk in, Jeanine's suicide is not on my mind, neither does the thought of it linger when it does come. I only record this because it is a curious thing that I sit now to write on the spot where my daughter died, where my great grief was born. Yet this spot is not debilitating. I sit here and write happily, or intensely. This is a miracle.

Still, there are moments when the memory of finding her dead invades my thoughts like a knife, cuts me quickly, and leaves a ragged edge, but I have learned how to bleed without making a mess.

Another anniversary of her death. A letter arrives from Steve, a youth worker at our church who was a good friend of Jeanine's:

> *I've been thinking about you guys every day this week and most especially today. Earlier this week I came across a large poster Jeanine had made. On it she had drawn a picture of my face in the shape of an egg, with her quote, "Steve, you're as sharp as an egg."*

I hadn't known about that poster. I'm so grateful for any such tidbits of information about Jeanine. I am given the gift of a memory when people tell me new things about her.

I am weeping this morning for Jeanine. It will not make sense to anyone else why when I tell it. I am reading Annie Dillard's *Holy the Firm*, and I come to the part where she tells of the moth that became a candle and burned for two hours "like a hollow saint, a flame-faced virgin gone to God," and tears fill my eyes. For some reason, the burning moth makes me think of Jeanine.

Just days before, I had dreamed about Jeanine. It was a positive dream. She had come back with no explanation as to how, but was not accusing me or John or anyone in relation to her suicide. She was sorry and knew she was forgiven. She was in fact radiant in her peace. I was completely filled up with joy to see her and touch her, to look in the face of my dear one. The dream was real enough that it colored my mood all that day with a sense of well-being.

What is life like for my loved ones who have died in Christ? I know where they are by faith. Can they see me? Hear me? Do they know what I'm thinking? Can my love still reach them? I know this much: they are surrounded by Love, the very personification of it. I think Emily Dickinson's poem[1] about the morning after death is right. I put my love away to be used again in another time and place. But the memories cannot be put away. They come bidden and unbidden, affecting each day according to their potency or poignancy.

Jesus said: "Blessed are you who weep now, for you shall laugh!" Here's something to look forward to: laughing together with Jeanine and all my dear ones in heaven.

I ask Joyella what she meant when, in those first few hours after Jeanine's suicide, she had said, "Now maybe we will be real." I had tucked this statement away all these many years. I wasn't able to think about their significance when she said it, but it comes to mind now, and I ask her about it. She isn't ready to answer, but a week later she gives me the following letter:

> *I knew immediately what I had meant when I said, "Now maybe we'll be real." But let me first tell you what I didn't mean.*
>
> *In no way had I meant that Jeanine's life kept our family from being a real family. I was only sixteen at the time of her death, and I had the misconception that our family was "too good to be true," or "real." I had even described our family to a friend at camp as plastic. Not that we were fake, but just too good. Nothing bad had ever happened to us, nor did any of us do anything very bad, although Jeanine's zest and spunk gave our family more color if not notoriety. The stories I heard at camp about my friends' families (their problems and tragedies) made me think I wasn't*

normal, that my family wasn't normal. I guess the pressure to fit in as a teen affected me more than I realized at the time. I really wanted to be "normal," like my friends. The irony in this is that the first year after Jeanine's death, when I was a senior in high school, I couldn't have felt more alone, more different or abnormal, even though now there was something that made my family look like my friends' families.

When someone dies whom we love dearly, it cuts us deeply. As our wound heals, it leaves a lasting scar. Revisiting the scar, touching it, reminds us we are "real." We are like everybody else. So, in a way, we have been made more "real," if that is possible, by Jeanine's death. But I can't help wondering how much more interesting our family would be if she were still here with us.

Like Joyella, I often think about what our family would be like if Jeanine were still here. What kind of aunt would she be to all her nieces and nephews? How would she be expressing herself in her dress, in conversations? Would she be dancing or painting? What would be occupying her great energy? Jeanine was the one in our family that might have worn the label *eccentric*. It's so much fun to have one in a family, especially if that eccentric one is anchored to the Lord of Life. And she was anchored. With flair! And now her faith is sight!

✳

We have to give sorrow time. Grief is a long walk through a corridor of painful as well as happy memories. I believe Jesus has already walked this corridor and walks it with me again. His life, which began in poverty and peril, was a long walk through misunderstanding and scorn toward his greatest pain, separation from his Father. And in that soul-separation that he willingly endured for my sake, his body was also being mutilated to death. He remained faithful to the end. And the end of his life on earth became my true beginning.

Joyella has a new daughter: Lorelei Jeanine Mischke. She is our eleventh grandchild, Joyella and Karl's third child, and Jeanine will never see her. Wait. Is that true? Don't I believe that all things good and beautiful in this life, like a new baby's downy head and the love that is shared in our family, contain eternity, are known in eternity? Yes.

CHAPTER SEVEN

Fear, Faith, and Reality

*And death and the grave were thrown into the lake of
fire. . . . then I saw a new heaven and a new earth. . . .
I heard a loud shout from the throne, saying, "Look,
the home of God is now among his people! He will
live with them, and they will be his people. . . . He
will remove all of their sorrows, and there will be no
more death or sorrow or crying or pain. For the old
world and its evils are gone forever.*

REVELATION 20:14; 21:1,3-4, NLT

Though it happens much less frequently, waves of shock, anxiety, and pain still wash over me if I let myself think about what Jeanine did — especially the physical aspects, the rope, the ladder. How could her mind lead her to that unspeakable act, that horrible death? I remember her beautiful body lying in a coffin, and then in a grave not far from our home. But at each rising of these waves, I am learning to replace those images with what I believe is true now: Jeanine is whole, alive somewhere with Christ, and healed of her needs, her depression, her sadness, and death itself. I think of her dwelling in eternal light and goodness and of being able to see the face of our great and loving God.

Acceptance and worship are acts of faith. My emotions and my mind respond with fear or doubt or rage because of the pain.

My emotions say:

> *God is not Love; he is a sadist*
>> *This is too horrible to bear*
>>> *It is unfair to have to experience this.*

But faith says:

> *You, God, are holy and good and loving*
>> *You do not make mistakes*
>>> *You are aware of this pain, yes, even allowing it, having designed it for my ultimate good. ·*
>>> *You are to be praised for whatever you are doing beyond my eyes' reach.*

One day I will see what God sees and know what he knows about my pain. I will wait. I will worship, and I will accept the pain that is pushing me closer to him.

✳

When John and I and our children (only three of them then; Jeanine was a baby) were on a ship sailing for the Philippines, I remember feeling so vulnerable out on those high and lonely seas, no other ships in sight for days. Our cabin was way below, on the next to the lowest deck. I called it "the belly of the whale." Lying on the rack at night I could hear the water rushing by, and I would think, *One little puncture in this huge tin can and . . .*

One evening, while lying there, I came upon Psalm 68:19 in my *Amplified Bible*: "Blessed be the Lord who bears our burdens and carries us day by day, even the God Who is our salvation! Selah. [Pause, and calmly think of that]!" I thought at the time, *Oh, I like this picture! This ship is not carrying us to the Philippines. It's really the Lord who is carrying us everywhere we go. We are safe in his arms.* Now, so many years later, I still feel this is true: My God is carrying me. He has carried me through all the years of traveling, living in two foreign countries, and through all the years of grieving. I am in good hands every single day of my life.

It is Easter, and we are all sitting around the table, singing, "He arose, He arose, hallelujah, Christ arose!" Our voices raised in song remind me that our friend, Bram, had prayed for us that "joyful noises would be heard in our house again."

When John and I were just starting our family, I found this promise in Isaiah 54:13:

"All thy children shall be taught of the LORD; and great shall be the peace of thy children." (KJV)

I don't know how to explain or defend my conviction that this verse was given to us as a personal promise. But I cannot shake the conviction. I still believe that our children are being taught by God and will be given his peace. It's what we have prayed for them all their lives. We have watched all four of them grow up into convinced and attractive followers of Christ. And so I can take comfort in the thought that Jeanine entered into the rest of her eternal life with Christ by her side. He took her and taught her as he had been doing all along. Now she knows exactly what that peace is like, that great peace Isaiah talks about and that Jesus himself promised would be ours.[1]

One day in the synagogue in Nazareth, Jesus stood up to read the Scriptures. He read from the Isaiah scroll,[2] and told his fellow Jews seated around him that the passage he had just read, written many centuries earlier, was all about him. It was his mission statement. He was sent to proclaim good news to the suffering ones, to bandage those with broken hearts, to give freedom to the prisoners. I believe this is what he continues to do until the final day when all pain and hate and need will be taken care of. All things will be set right and stay right. This is such good news; I tell it to myself every day.

I remember Jesus' message of hope and healing and choose to believe it, even when I am not feeling hopeful or healed. I have asked

God not only to heal me, but to fix things so that I and all the rest of us on this earth will never have to hurt again. And he says, "Wait."

Something new has been happening in my grief. I am missing Jeanine like never before. I am able to think of her as smiling, fun, busy, cute, and silly, without the dark cloud of her suicide hovering over my thoughts. So many sweet and laughing moments are returning. Then I feel sad because I think she will not be like this when I see her in heaven. She will be glorified and holy and so different.

But now I'm thinking that she will be all that she was meant to be, and I will recognize and give great praise to God for the true essence of her being, unencumbered by sin. I will be able to take full pleasure in her joy and creativity, the flavor of her humor, her love of life. I will see what God meant when he created her. And this will be true for every one of us when we look on each other in those heavenly days to come. We will know as we are known; we will see and understand our own beauty and the glorious beauty of everyone else. This is what heaven will be: seeing and touching and clinging to the One who made us for himself; and receiving each other in our full and true state of being, to enjoy for eternity.

When tears come and I feel the loss of my dear daughter, I remind myself that the tears are temporary, the hurt will dissolve, the lost will be found and given back to me in a way I never possessed before, never dreamed possible. Now on earth everything is spoiled to some degree by the sin in each of us and in the world's systems and cultures.

The creation itself suffers from the sin that is everywhere. In heaven, sin will be gone. We will see each other and God and all his holy and eternal purposes clearly. In that final and continual day, I will really know my daughter — and all my loved ones in Christ — in their true, sinless, everlasting glorious state.

I've heard it said that in every loss is a gift. Not something you can hear when the grief is fresh and splitting you apart. But now, after enough time has passed that I can think about such a thing, I believe it sounds like something God would do. Since he has said he bears our grief and carries our sorrows, and that he will make all things in our life on earth work together for good, receiving a gift out of grief fits in with these truths.

I bought something to remind me of this idea, that in every loss there is a gift. It's a terra-cotta angel, kneeling, wings cupped forward. I've placed it in the window next to my desk where I can see its sweet cherub face that reminds me so much of Jeanine's when she was small. This angel has a box in its hands, a present all tied up with ribbon, and it reaches out its hands to me. Every time I look at it, this little angel is offering me a gift. The angel's gift box has become a symbol to me of all that God has done for me in these years of loss and pain and restoration. It represents the comforting promise of God, that he will turn my mourning into dancing, take off my sackcloth, and give me a dress of gladness. The box represents the gift of writing that came out of my wound, out of the pain that drove me to write and to discover that I can. The gift in the angel's hands reminds me of God's gift of his presence. He has stayed very near me in my mourning, getting me up and going each day that I wanted to die. I'm reminded of the gift God has given of a greater delight in my salvation and in my Savior. I can get downright giddy sometimes just thinking about how much I love Jesus and how much Jesus loves me, how many ways he has shown his love. And so, whenever I sit down at my computer, I love to look at that little terra-cotta angel and thank God for all these gifts.

God has led me on a journey of humbling discovery. I see now that pride was at the heart of all my struggles. Grief alone is large, more than enough for anyone to bear. What pride conceived in me was heavy guilt and shame. At first, the fear had come along as part of the grief. But then fear attached itself to my guilt, and my struggles with shame were born. God has used these struggles to show me again how much he loves me. He helped me see my pride and understand the guilt and shame I carried because of Jeanine's suicide, and he has removed them from my mind. I know, in a way I couldn't before, what it means to be forgiven. I understand now that until I experienced God's forgiveness for what I perceived as a profound and far-reaching failure, I couldn't truly know the width and breadth of the mercy of God nor the depths of his unconditional love.

Here's another example of Jesus showing me his love: Today is another anniversary of Jeanine's death, and I go outside early to sit on the terrace to read and pray. I have my *Daily Light* with me — a devotional I haven't used for some time. I turn to the morning reading for July 24, and what I find is a precious surprise from the Lord. I believe God has seen to it that the verses to be read on this very date are exactly what I need to read. This from my journal entry:

Romans 12:12: "patient in tribulation . . ."

> Yes, Lord, I will be patient in this grief of mine and will
> not plead with you to make it go away.

Job 1:21 "The LORD gave and the LORD has taken away; may the name of the LORD be praised."

> Oh, God, help me to rest in this: that you have allowed
> Jeanine's death for your holy, yet hidden reasons. I do
> bless your name even though I feel anxious once in
> a while, about what you might yet allow. You are my
> God and I will trust you.

John 11:35; Isaiah 53:3,4: "Jesus wept . . ." "A man of sorrows, and acquainted with grief . . ." "Surely he has borne our grief, and carried our sorrows."

Jesus, you know what sorrow and tears feel like
because you carry my sorrow. And you have carried
me all my days. Knowing this makes my pain lighter
this morning. Thank you for your love that caused you
to suffer and die for me. I praise you, Lord, because
you are alive and Jeanine is with you, enjoying you,
knowing complete joy. Help me to remember this
when I am again overcome by sorrow. And thank you
for the particular comfort of these verses, chosen so
long ago and ordained by you to be read on this day
by me!

This kind of thing happens to me often. I come across the very verse
or thought that I need to hear, that speaks to my present state of mind,
as though God is saying to me, I know where you are; I know who you
are, and I AM HERE.

The most vile concoction we could imagine, death and all it entails,
all it affects, God swallowed it down, wrote the prophet Isaiah.[3] God
set a table with the best food and drink, proposed a toast to the death
of death, and then drank it all away. One day his own finger will wipe
away our tears and our disgrace. This is a personal God, a God who
longs to be intimate and tender with us. Isaiah says God told him to
write these things. He didn't make them up. I believe him.

*

At times I have wondered if I am self-deluded. I have even questioned the veracity of the Scriptures and at one time wondered whether it is possible to even know what is "true" truth. Over time, after much reading and discussion and thorough study of the Word and prayer, I have been able to put to rest some of my questions. Most likely, I will arrive in heaven with questions, but then I think I'll see all the answers in the blink of an eye. I remain convinced that God has made himself known to me. I not only believe in him, I know him. He resides not in my intellect, but in my very soul. To me and to everyone, to the weeping, needy, brokenhearted, and guilty, he reaches out his scarred hands and says, "Come."

Some may call my faith a crutch. I lean hard on God in whom I have come to trust. To my mind he continues to validate my trust. God says that because he loves me, he listens when I call out to him. I am confident that he will actually do something in response to my requests. I have much evidence of this in my journals — many recorded answers to specific prayers. He reads my heart, not my lips only. This is why I spill out all my thoughts to God, whether ordered prayer or not. Therefore I will believe what I know and refuse to admit the Enemy, who creeps about and tries to push into my thoughts, to impugn the character of God or strike fear in my heart. Bar the door. Sing and praise. Rehearse the truth:

The Lord God is my Strength, my personal bravery,
and my invincible army; He makes my feet like hinds'
feet and will make me to walk [not to stand still in

*terror, but to walk] and make [spiritual] progress upon
my high places [of trouble, suffering or responsibility]!
(Habakkuk 3:19, AMP)*

Here is what I have learned from my grief and loss so far:

First and foremost, my loss is only temporary. I believe in the resurrection of the body — Christ's body, my body, my daughter's body. A passage from John Donne's writings helps me focus on this ultimate truth:

> *All mankind is of one author, and is one volume; when one man dies, one chapter is not torn out of the book, but translated into a better language; and every chapter must be so translated; God employs several translators: some pieces are translated by age, some by sickness, some by war, some by justice; but God's hand is in every translation; and his hand shall bind up all our scattered leaves again, for that library where every book shall lie open to one another.*[4]

I also cherish this passage from Isaiah 26:19: "But friends, your dead will live, your corpses will get to their feet. All you dead and buried, wake up! Sing!" (MSG).

Second, losing a child is as crippling a wound as an amputation. We don't expect a person who has lost a leg to walk as though she had

123

two legs. Neither does a new limb grow back where the old one was. No other child or any other thing will replace the lost child. A prosthesis is available, but it doesn't look anything like the missing child. It may be a vigorous burrowing into work, or a new sense of the importance of the rest of the family, or of life itself. Or it may be patience or true grit. But some people don't want a prosthesis. They want to remain aware at all times of the space where the child was.

Third, reading and writing are ways toward healing. For me, God's Word has been primary and supreme among all the books I have ever read. The Bible is everything God promises it to be.[5] It spills truth deep into my mind and heart every time I read. It is delicious for meditation, medicine for my pain, and surgery for my sin. I will never regret all the time and effort it took to memorize hundreds of verses long before I knew how much I would need them. Someone has said that the time to build a house is not in the middle of a hurricane; nor is it feasible to go looking for weapons when you are in the thick of battle. The verses I began committing to memory when I was a teenager are foundational to my thinking about God and all aspects of my life. They are my stored-up artillery, tools against the whispered lies of the Enemy and of my own mind.

Grief and loss often bring confusion. For me, writing has helped me discover and clarify my true thoughts and feelings. In *Words Against the Cold*, Melanie Peter says something that resonates with my own experience. She said she wrote her way through the horror of her son's suicide. And in her writing she discovered joy again:

*Death magnifies life's colors. It washes over the world
and amplifies the message hidden in everything: Look.
Love. Now.*[6]

Pain is a reliable messenger to our physical bodies. It usually tells the
truth about physical injuries. But the pain of loss and grief may tell
lies to our mind, to our psyche. We may conclude, because of how
much we hurt, that God doesn't care, isn't fair, or perhaps isn't even
there. If we don't blame God for our misery, we blame each other. I
have learned that 85 percent of couples get divorced after the suicidal
death of their child. This is due to all the blaming. Now, John and I are
more tender, more alive to each other, more genuine in our words and
embraces. Our grief has married us like no ceremony could. We feel
indebted to God for keeping us well, strengthening our desire to love
each other better, deeper, more wisely.

I loathe the thought that I might sound trite when I speak of holy things.
I live in a constant state of awe — that I am still alive after dying, that
the trees outside my window know how to grow, that my husband and
children love me, that I can see and think and feel — these awesome
things are too heavy to carry around in my small heart. I need a bag
of some sort or a bottle to put my awe in, then pour it out carefully so
others will see the holy things as they spill out and will say, "Oh, it is
wonderful." Maybe writing is the bottle to contain my awe. I can pass

it around the circle for all to take a sip, and we will fall down on our faces.

I believe it is possible to live in the rubble of this warring world, to have a life full of pain and disappointment, and still rejoice. Jesus Christ walks beside me to help me through the minefields. And even in these dangerous and torn fields, he causes flowers to grow for me to pick. He gives me glimpses of the great things he has in store for me. I'm counting on this: Jeanine and I will both be healed and live in hilarity together forever.

I often imagine Jeanine coming to meet me when I get to heaven. She is smiling broadly and glowing all over, wearing a gown of shimmering rainbow threads, the bodice crossed with a gold and silver embroidered sash. A shining corona encircles her head. There is wisdom in her face and the same mischievous sparkle in her beautiful green eyes.

We hug and hug and we kiss each other's faces, and then as I begin to ask, "Why . . . ?" she says, "Oh, that! I was so full of sorrow when I arrived here because of all the pain I caused you. But it's all over, you know! As though it never happened! All the sad and hurtful and horrible things that have ever happened on earth are no longer true! Look around, Mom! This is the reality we were created for. Come with me," she says, laughing.

It Is Well with My Soul

This morning, I just happen to pull Abraham Kuyper's *Near To God* off the shelf, curious to see if I have ever really read it. I am delighted to find in its pages so many truths about the character and ways of God that I have been trying to absorb, through prayer and meditation, since Jeanine's death. As I read, I realize again that though I know myself to be wrapped up in God's loving arms, I must also know my God as the All-Powerful One, the Sovereign Lord. His plans and doings are so far above my understanding. I drop to my knees for a bit, in agreement and worship, and surrender afresh to my Almighty and All-Loving King.

Then I sit for a while longer in my Quiet Time chair, reading Kuyper, and I hear myself saying Yes, Yes, Yes, in the very room where I screamed No, No, No, so many years ago.

Fifteen years have now passed since Jeanine's death, and for the last few of them, I am enjoying the fact that my mourning has been turned into dancing. The sackcloth is gone. Color is permissible again in my wardrobe. I still continue to feel the hurt of grief at times. Whenever I look at photographs of Jeanine, a pang still shoots through me, a longing and a melancholy. And yes, sometimes the memory of finding her dead rises again in my thoughts. But these things are no longer threats. They have lost their power to intimidate. I know I am healing.

Just a few days ago, an envelope addressed to Jeanine came in the mail. It caused a momentary twinge in my chest to see her name in print, arriving so casually like that in the mailbox. The letter was from a national talent competition. I opened the folder and read, then smiled, then began to laugh at the offer: "YOUR TICKET TO THE STARS." Jeanine doesn't need this ticket. She's already there.

Opening

Now is the shining fabric of our day
Torn open, flung apart,
Rent wide by love.
Never again
The tight enclosing sky,
The blue bowl
Or the star-illumined tent.
We are laid open to infinity,
For Easter Love
Has burst His tomb and ours.
Now nothing shelters us
From God's desire —
Not flesh, not sky,
Not stars, not even sin.
Now glory waits
So He can enter in.
Now does the dance begin.

ELIZABETH B. ROONEY[1]

When We See Christ

Oft time the day seems long,
Our trials hard to bear.
We're tempted to complain,
To murmur and despair.

But Christ will soon appear
To catch His Bride away.
All tears forever over
In God's eternal day.

It will be worth it all when we see Jesus,
Life's trials will seem so small when we see Christ;
One glimpse of His dear face all sorrow will erase,
So bravely run the race 'til we see Christ.[2]

ESTHER KERR RUSTHOI

The LORD is my light and my salvation — so why should I be afraid? . . . The one thing I ask of the LORD — the thing I seek most —

is to live in the house of the LORD all the days of my life,

delighting in the LORD's perfections and meditating in his Temple.

For he will conceal me there when troubles come;

he will hide me in his sanctuary. . . .

Listen to my pleading, O LORD. Be merciful and answer me!

My heart has heard you say, "Come and talk with me."

And my heart responds, "LORD, I am coming."

I am confident that I will see the LORD's goodness

while I am here in the land of the living.

Wait patiently for the LORD.

Be brave and courageous.

Yes, wait patiently for the LORD.

PSALM 27:1,4-5,7-8,13-14 (NLT)

I will praise you, LORD, for you have rescued me.
You refused to let my enemies triumph over me.

O LORD my God, I cried out to you for help,
and you restored my health.

You brought me up from the grave, O LORD.
You kept me from falling into the pit of death.

You have turned my mourning into joyful dancing.
You have taken away my clothes of mourning and clothed me with
joy,
that I might sing praises to you and not be silent.
O LORD my God, I will give you thanks forever!

PSALM 30:1-3,11-12 (NLT)

Recommended Resources

BOOKS

Crabb, Dr. Larry, and Dr. Dan Allender. *Hope When You're Hurting*. Grand Rapids, Mich.: Zondervan, 1996.

Elliot, Elisabeth. *A Path Through Suffering*. Ann Arbor, Mich.: Servant, 1990.

Hewett, John. *After Suicide*. Westminster John Knox, 1980.

Schaeffer, Edith. *Affliction*. New Jersey: Revell, 1978.

Woltersdorf, Nicolas. *Lament for a Son*. Grand Rapids, Mich.: Eerdmans, 1987.

Yancey, Philip. *Where Is God When It Hurts*. Grand Rapids, Mich.: Zondervan, 1977, 1990.

WEBSITES

National Center for Injury Prevention and Control
www.cdc.gov/ncipc/factsheets/suifacts.htm.

More people die from suicide than from homicide in the United States. Every day, approximately eighty-six Americans commit suicide and 1,500 people attempt to commit suicide. It is the eighth leading cause of death for all Americans and the third leading cause of death for people ages fifteen to twenty-four. (From the Centers for Disease Control and Prevention website, February 2001. This website is a helpful resource for anyone wishing to learn more about suicide, its causes, symptoms, and prevention.)

National Strategy for Suicide Prevention
Also see: www.mentalhealth.org/suicideprevention. (This website has a suicide hotline number: 1-800-273-TALK.)

Notes

CHAPTER ONE

1. Psalm 56:3.
2. Psalm 31:7.
3. Phillip P. Bliss and Horatio G. Spafford, "It Is Well with My Soul," public domain.

CHAPTER THREE

1. John Hewett, *After Suicide* (Westminster John Knox, 1980), 52.
2. See Mark 6:45-51.
3. Isaiah 41:10.
4. Erma Bombeck, *The Sun*, Today sec., May 14, 1995.
5. See Hebrews 9:11-28.
6. See 1 John 1:9.
7. See Micah 7:19.
8. Robert Perkins, *Into the Great Solitude: An Arctic Journey* (New York: Henry Holt, 1991).

CHAPTER FOUR

1. See Proverbs 13:12.

2. "A single sexually exploitative incident in childhood, not necessarily penetration, but inappropriate touching or looking, causes exhaustive damage. . . . such boundary violations have severe, long lasting and widespread consequences." Anne Katherine, *Boundaries* (Fireside, 1993), 139.

3. The Amy Writing Awards (Lansing, MI: The Amy Foundation, 1994).

CHAPTER FIVE

1. James M. Houston, ed., *A Life of Prayer* by St. Teresa of Avila (Portland, Ore.: Multnomah, 1983).

CHAPTER SIX

1. See epigraph of chapter 1.

CHAPTER SEVEN

1. See John 16:33.
2. See Isaiah 61:1-3.
3. See Isaiah 25:8.
4. John Donne, excerpted from "Meditation" xvii, *The Complete Poetry and Selected Prose of John Donne* (New York: Random House, 1952), 440.

5. See Psalm 19:7-11.

6. Melanie Peter, *Words Against the Cold* excerpted from Rebecca McClanahan, *Write Your Heart Out* (San Francisco: Walking Stick, 2001), 79,103.

EPILOGUE

1. Elizabeth B. Rooney, "Opening" (Blue Mounds, WI: Brigham Farm Publishing) Used by permission of the Elizabeth B. Rooney Family Trust.

2. "When We See Christ," © 1941 Singspiration Music, a division of Zomba Enterprises, Inc. (ASCAP) (Administered by Brentwood-Benson Music Publishing). All rights reserved. Used by permission.

Author

Joyce Sackett and her husband John have served with the Navigators for more than forty years in the Netherlands, the Philippines, and Maryland. She has spoken internationally to women's groups and church conferences on topics relating to discipleship and spiritual growth. Tyndale House Publishers published her book, *In God's Garden* (more than 13,000 sold) as well as a perpetual devotional calendar she created, *Finding God in the Garden* (more than 11,000 sold). She has also had three articles published in *Discipleship Journal*. She and her husband John have three living children: Julie, Johnny, and Joyella, and they have eleven grandchildren.

LEARN TO BE GOD'S INSTRUMENT OF HEALING.

How to Help a Grieving Friend

When a friend's loved one dies, what do you say? Are you well-meaning but tongue-tied? Or are you able to provide meaningful comfort when no one else can?

Sadly, the one experience common to all humanity—death—is often the one we are least prepared to handle. This quick read will help caring people: speak healing words instead of tired clichés, recognize needs of the grieving, and comfort and empathize with heavy hearts.

Stephanie Grace Whitson
1-57683-677-0